# Women in Christianity

# Women in Christianity

Hans Küng

*Translated by John Bowden*

continuum
LONDON • NEW YORK

**Continuum**

The Tower Building
11 York Road
London SE1 7NX

370 Lexington Avenue
New York
NY 10017–6503

www.continuumbooks.com

First published 2001

**British Library Cataloguing-in-Publication Data**
A catalogue record for this book is available from the British Library.

ISBN   0 8264 5686 3

Sections of this book first appeared in Hans Küng, *Christianity: Its Essence and History*, SCM Press and Continuum 1995, and are included here by permission.

Typeset by Kenneth Burnley, Wirral, Cheshire
Printed and bound in Great Britain by Biddles,
Guildford and King's Lynn

# Contents

# Introduction

For most of the religions of the world women are a problem; from time immemorial they have been subordinate to men, second-class in the family, politics and business, with limited rights and even limited participation in worship. It is not only in Christianity that equal rights for women is a great unfulfilled concern.

But there is no doubt that whether women should have the same dignity and rights in Christianity as men is a particularly explosive issue. It is true that the emancipation of women in most recent times, especially in the Protestant, Anglican and Old Catholic churches, has made welcome progress. But in the Eastern Orthodox churches, which at any rate accept married priests (though not bishops), and above all in the Roman Catholic church, women are held down in an inferior status. At the parish level pioneering developments may have taken place, despite all the official obstacles, but the prohibition of women servers at mass and of the ordination of women to the diaconate and the priesthood still remains, as does the rigorously negative attitude to contraception, abortion and divorce, which in practice is more often than not at the expense of women. And Roman Catholic canon law, revised after the Second Vatican Council in the old spirit, is androcentric through and through, determined by males. As far as possible, women are kept away from professorial chairs in theology.

In all this Rome refers to 'tradition'. So in this book I shall investigate in particular the 2000-year history of women in Christianity, as far as this is possible within such a framework. The question is how a community structure which was originally quite different later developed the way it did.

I concede that the problem of the position of women in the church only dawned on me at the Second Vatican Council (1962–65), in which I took part as a theological adviser. The 1968 movement also helped the women's movement forward in the church. For me, Pope Paul VI's encyclical *Humanae Vitae* (1968) against contraception was the direct occasion for a wide-ranging 'Inquiry' under the title *Infallible?* (1970). The Vatican did not respond to this inquiry but punished me with an Inquisition (for which there was no legitimate basis) which on 18 December 1979 led to the withdrawal by the church of my permission to teach.

However, my new status at the University of Tübingen after 1980, independent of the faculty, gave me a great opportunity to pursue intensively areas of research which I had long cherished: world religions, world literature and finally also the role of women in Christianity. As early as the summer semester of 1981, with my then assistant Dr Anne Jensen, I held a seminar on Women and Christianity in which Dr Elisabeth Moltmann-Wendel of Tübingen and Dr Bernadette Brooten, now at Brandeis University, USA, took part. It was also through them that I decided to commission a two-part research project, supported by the Volkswagen Foundation, on Women and Christianity, which was carried out between 1982 and 1987 under the auspices of the Institute for Ecumenical Research at the University of Tübingen, which remained under my direction.

Chronologically, the project started from two poles: at one end the beginnings of Christianity and at the other the twentieth century. Since historians had hitherto hardly thought women's history worth transmitting, both these part-projects involved the laborious process of reconstructing the history of women at the time, as far as possible by women themselves. Despite the not inconsiderable difficulties, it proved possible to complete both part-projects successfully. The concluding report of the research project Women and Christianity in 1993 and the report of the Institute for Ecumenical Research both also contain information about the numerous lectures, seminars, working parties and other studies on the problem of Women and Christianity and the dialogue group on feminist theology (both can be obtained in manuscript form from the Institute for Ecumenical Research, Liebermeisterstrasse 18, 72076 Tübingen).

I made my own investigation of the role of women in Christianity in my book *Christianity: Its Essence and History*, the second volume of The Religious Situation of Our Time (ET 1995). I did this within the framework of an analysis of the different epoch-making overall constellations or paradigms of Christianity, which make it possible to view the present in the sight of the past:

- the Jewish-apocalyptic paradigm of earliest Christianity (P I);
- the ecumenical-Hellenistic paradigm of Christian antiquity (P II);
- the Roman Catholic paradigm of the Middle Ages (P III);
- the Protestant-Evangelical paradigm of the Reformation (P IV);
- the modern paradigm of reason and progress (P V);
- all this focussed on the beginnings of the ecumenical paradigm of postmodernity which are becoming visible (P VI).

In each of the different paradigms I dealt explicitly with the role of women. Women were mentioned in many different passages, sometimes amounting only to a paragraph or so, sometimes extending over several pages, and their experiences formed a subsidiary thread which ran right through the book. However, to identify them all would have been a major task for the reader interested in the question of the role of women in Christianity. Hence this book. In it I have brought together all the relevant passages, revised them, and provided them with

# 1 Women in Earliest Christianity

Women cannot assume any functions of leadership in the Catholic church and cannot be ordained 'priest', let alone 'bishop'. The main reason given for this is that Jesus, who for Christians is the Christ, did not choose any women as apostles. But it is very difficult now, after almost 2000 years, to discover anything about the daily life of the first generation of Christians. After all, we know hardly anything about the normal course of their lives, about their everyday worries, fears and joys. And who made up the earliest Christian community?

## Women's history too

If we want to understand the history of the earliest community we need to remember three things:[1]

1. This was not initially a history of Romans and Greeks, but a history of people who were born Jews. Though in the Hellenistic culture of Palestine some may have spoken Aramaic and others Greek, what they communicated to the whole church now coming into being was the world of Jewish ideas, Jewish language and Jewish theology. In this way they also left an indelible stamp on the whole subsequent history of Christianity – including the Gentile Christianity that was to come – down to the present day. The first overall constellation of Christianity (Paradigm I) was the Jewish–Christian paradigm.

2. Nor did historians mostly relate the history of an upper class, but the history of the lower classes: fishermen, farmers, craftsman, little people who normally have no chronicler. The first generations of Christians did not have any political power, nor did they strive for positions in the religious and political

establishment. They formed a small, weak, and discredited group on the periphery of the society of the time, under considerable pressure.

3. Most important of all, however, from the beginning Christianity was not just a movement made up of men; its history also includes the women who followed Jesus. Jesus' practice of calling women, too, to follow him was unconventional and undermined the existing patriarchal structures.

## Jesus – friend of women

In the time of Jesus women counted for little in society. As in some cultures even today, they had to avoid the company of men in public. Contemporary Jewish sources are full of animosity towards women, who according to the Jewish historian Josephus are in every respect inferior to men.[2] Husbands are advised not to talk much even with their own wives, far less with the wives of others. Women withdrew from public life as much as possible. In the temple they had access only to the Court of Women. And their duties in offering prayer were identical to those of slaves.

However, regardless of the question how much of the biographical detail in the Gospels is clear, the evangelists have no inhibitions about talking of Jesus' relations with women. According to them, Jesus dissociated himself from the customary exclusion of women. Not only does Jesus show no contempt for women; he is amazingly open towards them. Women accompany him and his disciples from Galilee to Jerusalem. We are given the names of many of them: Joanna, Susanna, Mary the mother of James and Joses, Salome and 'many other women', first and foremost Mary of Magdala.[3] Jesus showed personal affection towards women.[4] The group of disciples, which travelled around without possessions and had no fixed abode, was given effective support by women and the families of sympathizers, like those of Martha and Mary.

It is indeed the case that Jesus chose only men for the narrower group of the Twelve, which was to represent the people of twelve tribes in the end-time. But originally the twelve were not the only ones to be called 'apostles'.[5] The apostles, those sent out to proclaim their belief in Jesus' resurrection, form a relatively larger group[6] which could also have included women; it was the evangelist Luke more than a generation after Jesus who first identified 'the Twelve' with the apostles. However, women clearly play a significant role in the ongoing looser group of Jesus' disciples. These women disciples remained faithful to their master to the end, stood by the cross and observed the burial. The Twelve, one of whom had betrayed Jesus, had already fled.[7]

Sayings of Jesus which are apparently hostile to the family[8] are to be seen in this context. Anyone who for him is a brother or sister belongs in the 'family of God', which consists of those who do the will of the Father. For them, ties of blood are secondary and the relationship between the sexes loses its significance. However, Jesus of Nazareth, although he himself was un-married, did not make celibacy a condition of discipleship. Jesus can provide no legitimation for a law of celibacy, just as the Hebrew Bible nowhere praises the unmarried state. The apostles were married and remained so (Paul regarded himself as an exception).[9] However, the position of women in the society of the time, which was weak both socially and legally, was consid-erably enhanced by Jesus' prohibition of divorce (in Judaism only a man could draw up a letter of separation).[10] This prohibi-tion too – in Matthew the 'case of adultery' is given as an exception – has a specific focus; it no more excludes failure and forgiveness than do other commandments.

Jesus addressed God tenderly as 'Father', 'Dear Father'. But in doing so he did not intend to stress the masculine side of God. Using the name Father in addressing God does not denote any sexual differentiation in God: God cannot be claimed solely for the male sex. God is not at the same time male: in the Hebrew

Bible God also has feminine, maternal traits. Accordingly, the address 'Father', when used of God, is a patriarchal symbol (an analogy) of the trans-human, trans-sexual reality of God, who is also the origin of all that is feminine and motherly; it cannot in any way be used as the religious basis for a paternalistic society.

## Women in the Jewish–Christian Jesus movement

According to present-day research, there can no longer be any question that women played a considerably more important role than is directly indicated in the New Testament sources, not only among the disciples of Jesus, but also in earliest Christianity. We are above all indebted to the German-American New Testament scholar Elisabeth Schüssler Fiorenza for having investigated the New Testament material from a 'feminist theological perspective'. Her investigation confirms that in the early Jewish–Christian Jesus movement there was a 'praxis of equality and the involvement of all, both male and female disciples':

> The majority of them were not rich, like the Cynic philosophers who could reject property and cultural positions in order 'to become free from possessions'. Rather, they were called from the impoverished, starving and 'heavy laden' country people. They were tax collectors, sinners, women, children, fishers, housewives, those who had been healed from their infirmities or set free from bondage to their evil spirits. What they offered was not an alternative lifestyle but an alternative ethos: they were those without a future, but now they had hope again; they were the 'outcast' and marginal people in their society, but now they had community again.[11]

How far, though, women were active as charismatic itinerant preachers in the early Jewish–Christian community can only be conjectured. Historically this can no more be verified than the thesis that women were decisive for the extension of the Jesus movement to non-Jews.[12] So we should be very restrained in concluding 'historical leadership roles'[13] or even 'leading positions for women'[14] from individual texts (e.g. the Syro-Phoenician woman in Mark 7.24–30). This also applies to the role of Mary Magdalene, who might have been the most significant female figure from Jesus' immediate circle.

None of this, however, detracts from the important recognition that the activity of Jesus called to life a community of disciples who were equals, and this also represents a criticism of the situation in the church today. And if explicit criticism of patriarchy was no essential concern of the Jesus movement, Elisabeth Schüssler Fiorenza is still right:

> No one is exempted. Everyone is invited. Women as well as men, prostitutes as well as Pharisees. The parable of the 'Great Supper' jolts the bearer into recognizing that the kingdom of God includes everyone. It warns that only those who were 'first invited' and who then rejected the invitation will be excluded. Not the holiness of the elect but the wholeness of all is the central vision of Jesus. Therefore, his parables also take their images from the world of women. His healings and exorcisms make women whole. His announcement of 'eschatological reversal' – many who are first will be last and those last will be first – applies also to women and to their impairment by patriarchal structures.[15]

## No patriarchal hierarchy

That Jesus himself relativized the 'fathers' and their traditions, called women, too, into his group of disciples, and even expressed his high esteem for children, shows that patriarchal hierarchies cannot have appealed to him. Nor did he make, for example, celibacy a condition of discipleship. The church of the Jewish–Christian paradigm (P I) could have been called democratic in the best sense of the word (at any rate it was not aristocratic or monarchical): a community in freedom, equality, and brotherhood and sisterhood. For this church was:

- not a powerful institution, not a Grand Inquisition, but a community of free people;
- not a church of classes, races, castes or ministries, but a community of those who in principle were equal;
- not an empire under patriarchal rule with a cult of persons, but a community of brothers and sisters.

However, we should note here that although all members of this early church in principle had an equal status, and in principle had the same rights and duties, this did not mean a uniform egalitarianism, a co-ordination and uniformity which levelled out the multiplicity of gifts and ministries. On the contrary: the earliest Jerusalem community in which, according to Luke, people were of 'one heart and one soul',[16] showed individuals opposed to one another, a variety of positions, differentiated functions and provisional structures

## Provisional structures

On the basis of the texts we cannot ignore the fact that from the beginning – despite the apocalyptic expectation of an imminent end – there were provisional structures in the community: above all the group of Twelve, but also the group of Seven whom the Acts of the Apostles calls 'Hellenists'. From this we can conclude that the community which followed Jesus will by no means have consisted only of Aramaic-speaking Jews, but also in no small degree of Greek-speaking Hellenistic Jews.

At any rate the conflict over the daily care of widows reported in Acts 6.1 seems to reflect a marked division in the earliest community between 'Hellenists' on the one hand and 'Hebrews' on the other. This division is further underlined by the fact that to all appearances other Jewish–Christian groups had their own synagogues and their own house communities in which scripture was read at worship in their own language – Hebrew or Greek. These Jewish–Christians who had Greek as their mother tongue (socially and culturally they came from the urban milieu of Hellenistic Diaspora Judaism and, because they were educated, were probably also more active in thinking about the implications of their faith) may have been led by the Stephen group ('the Seven', all of whom have purely Greek names). They were probably relatively independent of the group of apostles representing the 'Hebrews' ('the Twelve', who represented the twelve tribes of Israel). At the same time that means that 'the Seven' may well have been much more than simply welfare officers subordinate to the 'Twelve', as Luke's Acts of the Apostles reports a generation later. We should see them more as the 'governing body of an independent community' which was already engaged in active mission in Jerusalem at that time.

## Women as apostles and prophets?

Not just the Twelve, nor even the Seven, were apostles, but all those who were regarded as the original witnesses and messengers: those who proclaimed the message of Christ and founded and led communities as the first witnesses. We cannot tell whether the title apostle was also given to women in Jewish Christianity; things would be different in the Gentile–Christian sphere. But it is certain that right from the beginning in Jewish Christianity – and this is easily overlooked – there were not only prophets but also prophetesses: in addition to Agabus, Judas and Silas, mention is explicitly made in Acts of the four daughters of Philip.[17] Alongside them were evangelists and helpers of very different kinds, here too both men and women.

And what about offices in church? These various church ministries and callings were not given that name at this time. In fact in the New Testament secular terms for 'office' were avoided and with good reason. Why? Because such terms expressed a

# 2 Women in the Early Church

In communities, as a rule, people usually have a variety of tasks, ministries and functions, and already in the New Testament a whole series of functions can be distinguished. There are those who perform the functions of apostle, prophet, teacher, evangelist; those who preach and admonish; then, in auxiliary ministries, there are the deacons and deaconesses, those who distribute alms and care for the sick; widows serving the community; and finally, as the leaders of the community, the first converts, overseers, *episkopoi*, pastors and so on.

## Women apostles and prophets in Paul

All these functions in the community (and not just specific 'offices') were understood by Paul, about whose communities we have by far the best information, as gifts of the Spirit of God and the exalted Christ. Those who exercised such functions might feel themselves to be called by God to a particular ministry in the community. In Paul, such a gift of the Spirit is called briefly, in Greek, *charisma*. The Protestant exegete Ernst Käsemann[1] has strongly emphasized the charismatic dimension of the church in Paul: according to Paul, not only the extraordinary phenomena highly prized in present-day charismatic communities (like speaking in tongues and healing the sick) are charisms, gifts of the Spirit, but also quite everyday and as it were 'private' gifts and ministries like the gift of consolation, of admonition, of knowledge, of speaking wisdom, of discerning the spirits. They are not limited to a particular circle of persons. One cannot talk of either clericalism or enthusiasm in Paul. On the contrary, any ministry which in fact contributes to the building up of the community (permanent or temporary, private or public) is church ministry; and as a concrete ministry it has to be recognized and given its place. Thus any ministry, whether official or not, has its own kind of authority if it is performed in love for the benefit of the community.

There is no question that if the church of the Jewish–Christian paradigm (P I) can be called democratic in the best sense of the word, in that it is a community in freedom and equality, a community of brothers and sisters, this is probably even more the case with the Pauline communities, which mark the beginning of the Hellenistic paradigm (P II). Nowhere is this made more impressively clear than in the sentence which Paul writes to his community in Galatia: 'For as many of you as were baptized into Christ have put on Christ (as a garment). There is neither Jew nor Greek, there is neither slave nor free, there is neither male nor female; for you are all one in Christ Jesus.'[2] Indeed, there can be no doubt of this: in his letters Paul addresses women as his *synergoi*, which literally means 'fellow workers', i.e. 'colleagues'.

We have only to read the greetings at the end of the letter to the Romans to see how many women were actively involved in the proclamation of the gospel: ten of the twenty-nine prominent people addressed here are female.[3] First we have Phoebe, who was on an official mission for the church of Cenchreae. She is called *diakonos*, which suggests that she was the leader of a house community.[4] Junia is particularly important; Paul even describes her, along with Andronicus, as 'distinguished among the apostles' who had already 'confessed Christ' before him.[5] Apostle (in Greek there is no feminine form) is the highest title Paul can bestow. Moreover, as Ulrich Wilckens has rightly pointed out, Junia may have been one of the 'numerically limited group of those leading missionaries who had extraordinary authority as "apostles" and to whom Paul himself was only added later. This is a wider circle than the group of the Twelve.'[6]

At all events the general evidence is unambiguous: many of

the women mentioned by Paul are called 'hard workers' for the gospel – a favourite word of Paul's for denoting apostolic dedication.[7] According to the letter to the Philippians women like Eudonia and Syntyche – with exactly the same status as Paul and his other male fellow-workers – 'fought for the gospel'.[8] Their dispute, to which Paul alludes, was evidently so important to him that he entreats them to come to an agreement. Prisca, who with her husband Aquila is mentioned several times in Paul's correspondence, also has a special status.[9] The couple may have had a house in Ephesus in which they gathered a house community,[10] and we may also assume that later they led a group in their house in Rome. That Prisca is usually mentioned before her husband Aquila shows that she was particularly important as a missionary and founder of a church.

We have already seen that the activity of women prophets is also attested; there are no objections to them, even if the New Testament does not name any particular individual in the Gentile–Christian sphere. Paul also knows such prophetesses. Certainly he wants to make women uttering prophecies wear veils in worship, but at the same time he confirms their right to free speech in the community assembly: 'Any woman who prays or prophesies with her head unveiled dishonours her head.'[11] So there can be no doubt that the community as Paul sees it, and which according to the letter to the Ephesians 'is built upon the foundation of the apostles and prophets',[12] was also a church of women apostles and women prophets. So to sum up, we may say with Elisabeth Schüssler Fiorenza:

> The Pauline literature and Acts still allow us to recognize that women were among the most prominent missionaries and leaders in the early Christian movement. They were apostles and ministers like Paul, and some were his co-workers. They were teachers, preachers, and competitors in the race for the gospel. They founded house churches and, as prominent patrons, used their influence for other missionaries and Christians.[13]

## Conflicts over the status of women

But already in Corinth the first conflicts were brewing over women preaching in public, and even Paul is ambivalent here: although he defends the right of women to speak, in insisting on the veil he takes over arguments from an anti-feminist polemic of early Judaism.[14] He gives these a christological backing: the man is the head of the woman, and Christ is the head of the man.[15] A few decades later, in some texts women are then totally prohibited from even speaking in the community: the notorious saying 'Women are to keep silent in church' has even been manipulated into the selfsame letter to the Corinthians,[16] although three chapters earlier Paul had expressly confirmed women's right to make prophetic utterances. The prohibition against speaking then finds its sharpest expression in the so-called Pastoral Epistles, which, while claiming the authority of the apostle to the Gentiles, come from a later time: 'Let a woman learn in silence with all submissiveness. I permit no woman to teach or to have authority over men; she is to keep silent.'[17]

All this shows that the early Christian baptismal confession of the unity of man and woman 'in Christ' which Paul quotes in Galatians was not really put into practice everywhere. There were also forces at work which always sought to limit the equal treatment of Jews and Greeks, freemen and slaves, men and women. This tendency finally gained the upper hand, so that gradually even the women mentioned in the New Testament came to be forgotten, or their significance was played down. Thus over the centuries in the Latin-speaking West the Junia in Romans who is distinguished with the title apostle was turned into a man, 'Junias'.[18] Thus, too, later the apostle's disciple Thecla of Iconium, who preached and baptized (however, she is not mentioned in the New Testament), was transformed into an ascetic recluse.[19] And already in the Gospel of John, Mary Magdalene, who in the Synoptic Gospels is still depicted as a leading figure among the women from Galilee, is no longer men-

tioned as the first of the women under the cross. She is dis-
placed by Mary the mother of Jesus,[20] who, according to the
Synoptic Gospels, strikingly enough was not to be found there.
Granted, in the Gospel of John in particular Mary Magdalene
then becomes the 'first witness to the resurrection',[21] and consequently is later even honoured with the title 'apostle of the
apostles'.[22] But as time went on, people no longer wanted to
draw conclusions from this for the right of women to preach the
gospel as men did. Indeed, the question of the status of women
shows an increasing repression of the original 'democratic' and
'charismatic' structures to be found at the beginning of
Christianity. The process of institutionalization which now
ran its course increasingly favoured men – except perhaps in
the Gnostic movement in the second century.

## Gnosticism: an opportunity for women

Syncretism was in keeping with contemporary trends and in
the interest of the Roman state, and a slogan of the time –
already in Paul's Corinth – was *Gnosis*: 'Knowledge'. But
Gnosis was more than a slogan. Gnosis (also called Gnosticism)
was one of the great religious movements of late antiquity
which promised to an élite a redemptive knowledge of the mysteries of human beings, the world and God.

But even the most benevolent interpreters of Gnosticism
cannot overlook its danger for Christianity: quite untroubled by
the unmythological and historical origin of Christianity, indeed
despising the simple church faith of mere 'believers', known as
the 'pistics', Christian 'Gnostics', 'knowers' – all the Valentini-
ans, Basilidians, Ophites (snake worshippers) and rival
subordinate and parallel groups – attempted with the help of
every possible myth, image, metaphor, symbol and ritual to
transform the message of Christ rooted in history into a
mythical theology. They promised a radical spiritualization and
liberation from earthly fetters and displayed a tendency which

was usually hostile to the world and ascetic (sometimes even libertine, though there is no evidence of that at Nag Hammadi). Was there not thus a danger that the original Jewish–Christian faith would disappear in the undertow of a Hellenistic syncretism which swallowed up everything?

. The danger of syncretism was real: was Christianity at this early stage in some circumstances to accept more than one God and redeemer? Was it also to accept true Gods and redeemers from other religions? Was it to accept God the Mother as well as God the Father? And instead of faith in Father, Son and Spirit, was it to accept a Trinity of Father, Mother (or Wife) and Son? Was it to accept a mythicization of the couple, so that the heavenly Wisdom as universal mother also had to stand as consort alongside the heavenly Christ? For example, might one assume, against what was to be read in the Gospels (read aloud in the liturgy of the mainstream church) that a spirit-man Christ (who was probably only inserted into some Gnostic texts at a later stage) could not suffer at all and was not even crucified?

In these circumstances, the existence of the Gnostics within the communities of the mainstream church proved increasingly difficult. No wonder that these people who understood themselves as the 'elect', children of 'light', the 'spiritual', the 'free', indeed as God's 'unchangeable family', as 'seeds' from the world of light and therefore 'the family of Seth', also formed their own communities. We can only guess what these communities might have been like, made up of an educated élite (the 'knowers' and leaders) on the one hand and a relatively uneducated group on the other: they were evidently more 'cultic associations' with arcane discipline than hierarchically organized churches.

It is certain that women[23] could perform functions among the Gnostics which were forbidden them in the official church: not only as prophetesses, teachers and missionaries, but also as liturgists in prayers, hymns and sermons, and also in baptism and the eucharist – that is, in so far as these rites were celebrated at all among the Gnostics, who were hostile to the cult in principle. At any rate baptism and the eucharist are attested in a Nag Hammadi fragment, as similarly are washings, anointings with oil, meals and rites for the dying. The notion that the redeemed are brothers and sisters may have served as the ethical basis of communal life: brotherhood and sisterhood in terms not of the shaping of worldly society, but of redemption from worldly existence.

However, a warning must be issued here against any idealization of Gnosticism at the expense of the community church. Alongside the equal status for woman in practice and in the cult, in some texts there is also a marked devaluation of women, indeed a castigation of the feminine and a rejection of marriage. In view of the ideal of bisexuality which in part is attributed even to the supreme being, blame for the separation of the sexes is often foisted on the woman (Eve). Indeed, according to some texts the woman has to be made man in order to be able to enter the '*pleroma*'.

## Women: the losers in history

There is no doubt that the Gentile–Christian church stood up to its first great external threat (persecutions) as it did to its first great internal crisis (Gnosticism). But since the fundamental work of Walter Bauer on orthodoxy and heresy in early Christianity[24] we know that the early Christian authors cannot so easily be divided into winners and losers, 'orthodox' and 'heretics' – if we adopt a strictly historical perspective. For today we know that the history of theology and the church, too, was predominantly written by the victors at the expense of the losers – along dogmatic or church-political lines. The losers in this kind of traditional church history are not just individual 'heretics' who have been rehabilitated by more recent historiography.[25] Whole areas of Christianity were the losers, like the Jewish Christians who, as we saw, for the most part were already being regarded as heretical in the second and third centuries. And the whole of the other half of Christianity, women, were losers, as we shall now see in more detail.

For all too long, traditional historiography has neglected the question of women as subjects of history. However, while the sources for the situation of women in earliest Christianity were already scanty enough, the situation is almost hopeless when we come to the Christianity of the early church. Certainly there are numerous statements by numerous church fathers 'about' women, but there are very few testimonies from women themselves – all in all only four works certainly written by women, all extremely different.[26] Or there are scattered and fragmentary references in texts composed by men, most of which are about other questions.

It has constantly been pointed out how many statements there are, particularly in the Greek church fathers, about the equal status of men and women before God: both are created in the image of God; both have the same ethical and spiritual capacities and duties; women are the first witnesses to the resurrection of Jesus. But on the other hand it cannot be denied that at a very early stage in Christianity – and not just in monasticism, though it was especially encouraged there – there was an antipathy to the human body which devalued women. Even a theologian as open to the world as Clement of Alexandria, who defended the equality of man and woman in the spirit of the Stoa, who had reservations about lifelong sexual continence, and who in no way wanted to regard celibacy as the higher ideal for Christians, argues for the subordination of the woman to the man. And with him there were countless bishops and theologians who constantly argued that women are inferior and should be excluded from church offices.

The history of the interpretation of the New Testament and the writings of the early church speaks its own language here. And on the 'women's question' in particular it becomes clear how much the interpretation of the facts is dependent on the particular ideological interest of a time. For a long while it was taken for granted that the subordination of women desired by the church was legitimated by divine revelation and sacred tradition, and this is still the position of some clergy in Rome, England and elsewhere – for ever yesterday's men. Today in the Christian world the tendency is, rather, to emphasize the positive statements about women in the church fathers and credit Christianity with a special contribution to the emancipation of women. Who is right?

At a very early stage the historian Klaus Thraede produced a concise survey of the material and drew attention to the decisive point: while the number of women in the communities in the second and third centuries seems to have been high, the church's equal treatment of women did not take account of this; rather, orthodox theologians attempted to stem the emancipation of women: 'Here, the more ascetical ideals became established in orthodox Christianity, the more it thought in a markedly old-fashioned way, which included a stereotyped criticism of cosmetics, hygiene and fashion . . . Contrary to a view widespread today, that Christianity furthered the emancipation of women, in its basic ethical attitude the mainstream church lagged far behind the real conditions of the period of the empire (in part even behind philosophical doctrines: the legacy of the pre-Christian moral preaching which was hostile to women predominates).'[27]

However, in order to have some understanding not only of the testimonies of the church fathers 'about' women, but also of the world in which women of the time lived and the way in which they understood themselves, we need to read the whole of 'patristic' literature, sometimes 'against the grain', and this is a difficult business. For even if we limit ourselves to the canons and church orders of the early church, ascetic treatises and hagiographical narrative writings, historical detection requires laborious and detailed work if we are to reconstruct how women really lived and how they understood themselves. The

Catholic theologian and historian Anne Jensen did pioneer work here in the context of the Tübingen research project 'Women and Christianity', and I can now use her main findings as a basis.[28] She was rightly concerned to overcome a traditional way of writing church history in which the 'view of the victors' dominates, in other words, an approach which uncritically takes over the boundaries which later centuries drew between the mainstream church and the 'heretics'.[29]

A comparison of the four normative histories of the early church, by Eusebius, Socrates, Sozomen and Theodoret, which Anne Jensen undertook for the first time,[30] already produced a clear result. In the account of the first three centuries by Eusebius, Bishop of Caesarea, around 325, we learn essentially more about the active participation of women in church life than in the three later authors, who report on the fourth and fifth centuries; in them we can note a clear tendency to marginalize women and make them anonymous. Strikingly, there are no reports in these church histories of autonomous women ascetics, whose great spiritual authority is described in other sources; by contrast, in Eusebius and the witnesses mentioned by him there are no deaconesses or their predecessors, no 'widows' recognized by the church in the service of the communities. But the fact that in later centuries one increasingly comes upon these ordained women office-holders in no way indicates a revaluation of active community work by women. Rather, a critical comparison with other sources shows that the establishment of the diaconate is to be seen as a tendency towards restrictive measures, even if it allows women some freedom of action in the church sphere. The same applies to the communities of 'virgins' which were formed by ascetics living a determinedly autonomous life, who increasingly came under episcopal supervision.

## To be rediscovered: women martyrs, prophets, teachers

After this general panorama, which was produced from histories of the early church, Anne Jensen also investigated individual groups of women who were particularly important in the early period of Christianity. The evaluation of reports of women martyrs[31] led her to conclude that while here, too, men predominate numerically, when women are mentioned they are depicted on an equal footing. Special attention needs to be paid to the record of the trial at Lyons in 177, contained in the Acts of the Martyrs, at the centre of which stands the slave girl Blandina, and the trial in Carthage (203) of Perpetua and Felicitas, on which Perpetua herself made notes during her imprisonment – one of the few testimonies to come from a woman at this time. The theological analysis of these documents demonstrates that women confessors, who risked their life in bearing witness to Christ no less than male confessors, were recognized as witnesses empowered by the Spirit. It was recognized that many members of the community had a right in times of persecution to receive lapsed Christians back into church communion. However, here we must be careful not to generalize: the egalitarian practice of individual groups of this 'confessing church' was only partially representative of the Christianity of the time.

In the early period of Christianity, prophetesses above all were regarded as witnesses empowered by the Spirit.[32] Here we encounter 'Montanism', a prophetic movement in second-century Phrygia which is associated with the names of the prophetesses Prisca and Maximilla. Virtually no trend in early Christianity has been so vilified and contested by an uncritical reading of later polemical texts than this 'new prophecy' – the name chosen by the movement, which developed into an independent church. However, thorough investigation of the early sources to discover the facts which underlie the polemic, and investigation of the few prophetic sayings which have been handed down, demonstrate that the modern designation 'Montanism' is wrong in two respects. First, it puts Montanus, the 'advocate' of the prophetesses, who gave them organizational support, at its centre rather than the spiritual women leaders of this movement. Secondly, and above all, it suggests a 'supreme head' for the movement who did not exist, since this movement in particular had a charismatic ethos with an egalitarian orientation. According to the extant sources, Prisca must have been the most significant personality of the 'new prophecy'. So here again we discover traces of a real practice of putting men and women on the same level in second-century communities. It is particularly striking that the activity of women as such becomes the object of criticism only in later polemic.

We discover just how fruitful it is to get beyond the 'perspective of the victors' in historiography if we investigate those women who were active in public in the community as teachers.[33] These must be understood against the background of movements especially connected with Gnosticism. Then it is possible to rediscover and evaluate Philoumene, a woman theologian almost forgotten today, but a significant one. She was head of a school in Rome in the second century and was a rival to no less a figure than Marcion. Occupying a moderate position between Gnosticism and the mainstream church, this teacher and prophet argued for a radically spiritual understanding of resurrection (not bodily), but without falling victim to a christological docetism. The notion that creation was the work of a demiurge certainly puts the good creator God at a distance from evil in the world, but does not lead to a radical dualism in which the world and matter are rejected as evil. So Philoumene was an important pioneer of the new synthesis between Jewish-biblical and Hellenistic-philosophical thought in late antiquity. But already in the fourth century, though far more in modern church history, the initiator of this school came under the shadow of her disciple Apelles, who preserved her preaching in writing and disseminated her teaching.

If we look at the results of research into women so far, the picture proves to be more complex than was perhaps expected. As with the work of Elisabeth Schüssler Fiorenza on the New Testament period, Anne Jensen's investigation also brings out contradictions:

- Women were more intensively involved in the dissemination of Christianity than the sources with their androcentric colouring at first give us to understand.
- At the same time, forces are at work everywhere which seek to prevent putting the sexes on an equal footing. Resistance to the consistent realization of an egalitarian ethos increases.

## Alternative forms of life for women

Anne Jensen was able to show that many measures which repressed the activity of women in the church at first had little success, since the Hellenistic Roman women who became Christians were not going to submit to discipline lightly. Though they had no access to political office, they were never-theless 'e-mancipated' in the literal sense: they were no longer under the manus (= 'hand', in the sense of power and protec-tion) of a spouse, but were free partners and economically independent to the degree that they had personal resources. So it was quite possible for women of the upper class to lead their own lives even within marriage. This explains why there are no indications in the sources that women hoped for an improve-ment of their condition as women by going over to Christianity.

Nevertheless, many women who were still single or had again become single decided against a traditional family life. So widows now played a significant role in the communities, as soon also did virgins, young women who had resolved from the start not to get married. Certainly a preference for continence was a universal phenomenon of the time, and thus specific neither to women nor to Christians. Yet these voluntarily celibate Christian women created organizations within the churches which are unique in contemporary Hellenism on this scale. In Christianity, alternative forms of life were now possible for a large group of women, forms of life which were not defined by biological determination. This institution-alization guaranteed women both material provisions and a high degree of social recognition. Thus the association of women with a particular social role was broken through and transcended. Doubtless the Christian women themselves created the foundations for these new forms of female life, and even today the alternative to marriage provided by convents, communities and associations of very different kinds is chosen essentially more by women than men. This new understanding of femininity, which freed itself from the exclusively biological determination of women, was an essential contribution to the history of emancipation.

## The shadow sides

However, this relativizing of the old role of the sexes brought problems of its own. For only through radical renunciation of sex was it possible for women to escape their biological deter-mination. And the woman who was neither a spouse nor a mother found social recognition in Christianity only if there was a religious and ascetic basis to this renunciation of sex. It was at this point that conflicts arose. Why? Evidently women who decided against the usual family life had different motives. For some, renunciation of sex at the same time meant a radical rejection of a worldly life, which was accepted and indeed finally praised on the church side. For others, sex was renounced simply to make it possible to take on other tasks free from biological constraints. But this was regarded by many as grasping at 'male' roles and the claim to leadership associated with them. While it could be tolerated in exceptional cases, as a mass phenomenon it was evidently thought increasingly more threatening by the church. So there are ambivalent reactions:

The 'positive' solution was the theological construct of the 'sexless' parthenos (the virgin woman or man), in other words the radical transcending of sex, which in theory was to lead to completely equal rights for women and men and in practice to an open brotherly and sisterly pattern of behaviour. For this model, a hierarchy of the sexes was inconceivable. So here the effort to overcome the sexual is not a priori to be identified with hostility to sex, though this could easily develop.

The 'negative' solution consisted in a specific form of contempt for women which was soon to become dominant in part of the ascetic movement. Anxiety about a drive which might possibly get out of control produces the hostile image of the seductress. This tendency begins increasingly to become established in the early church and leads to the principle of the separation of the sexes.

Thus a fatal interplay begins: in the imperial church, hierarchical thought increasingly suppresses the original Christian efforts at egalitarianism and leads to asceticism; conversely, increasing sexual pessimism even outside the monastery has an effect on church and society. Even unmarried women who wanted to play an active part in church life were finally almost completely eliminated from the clerical state. In defining the relationship between the sexes, hierarchical thought finally proved victorious – and only in the free churches of modern times did the egalitarian ethos again gain ground within Christianity. So can we speak of an emancipation of women through Christianity in the time of the early church?

## Were women emancipated through Christianity?

According to Anne Jensen, two current theses which fundamentally represent only apologetic feminist or conservative anti-feminist variants of the same false conclusion prove to be wrong: 1. the heresies were better disposed towards women than the mainstream church; 2. because women were more prone to heretical trends, the church had to forbid women to teach. Rather, a precise investigation of the sources leads to the conclusion that even in the contested 'heretical' churches a consistent egalitarian ethos could not maintain itself for long. That means that in late antiquity the demarcation line between hostility to women and openness towards them was identical neither with the frontiers of religion nor with the confessional frontiers.

It is also important to note that in traditional Christian apologetic the charge of hostility to sexuality is readily made against the pagans, on the basis of the biblical heritage. But that of course also makes things too easy. For early Christianity did not just take over from Hellenism a tendency to shun the world. With its original expectation of an imminent end of the world and the judgment of the world, Christianity considerably heightened any aversion to the world. This becomes particularly clear in the ideal of continence: whereas in late antiquity outside Christianity the decision for an ascetic life could ultimately remain a matter of individual preference, in the teaching of the church, celibacy in time took on a pre-eminence grounded in salvation history. This led directly to a devaluation of sexuality and indirectly to a devaluation of women, who, in so far as they did not live continent lives, were increasingly defined in a one-sided biological way as sexual beings.

Certainly there is no disputing the fact that the ideal of humanity in antiquity already emphasized that all human beings, men and women, slaves and masters, poor and rich, had the same dignity. So an alliance between the Christian and the ancient egalitarian ethos might have been expected. Why did historical developments turn out differently? Further factors must have been in play. For the expansion of Christianity alone cannot explain the increasing discrimination against the female sex in the history of Western Christianity.

So it seems more appropriate first of all to ask a neutral question. What prevented a true emancipation of women in the early church? Among the different factors involved here, three seem especially important, and unfortunately they now came increasingly to determine the Hellenistic paradigm of the early church (P II):

- The establishment of hierarchical structures: as in the Roman empire, so too in the churches, there was rivalry between an egalitarian ethos and political power-interests; the principle of equality primarily asserted itself only in the private sphere, whereas male domination became established especially in the sacramental sphere.
- Hostility to sexuality: this does not derive from Christianity, but is a general phenomenon in late antiquity; however, it became particularly developed in Christianity.
- Devaluation of education: education was a Hellenistic ideal which, though initially not neglected in Christianity, was later in part openly despised – especially for women. This made a major contribution towards perceiving women exclusively as 'body'.

### Tradition as an argument today

So how are we to evaluate this tradition of hostility to women, compared with the basic attitude of Jesus, the Jewish Christian communities in Palestine and also the Gentile Christian communities with a Pauline stamp? The evidence is clear: vertical hierarchies increasingly began to get in the way of the brotherliness and sisterliness which was the stamp of Jesus and the early Christians. Hostility to sex was taken over from ancient tradition and propagated at the expense of women, although nothing of the kind can be discerned in the preaching of Jesus, which at most shows a marked relativization of marriage and family in favour of the kingdom of God. Education as a positive value hardly appears in the preaching of Jesus: one can enter into the kingdom of God without being educated. But Paul is already an educated Jewish Christian, as are the (anonymous) authors of such highly theological and highly educated letters as the letters to the Ephesians and the Hebrews. But equally, those concerned to devalue education cannot appeal to Jesus either, not to mention Paul and other authors. In particular, any devaluation of education which results in a 'ban on teaching' for women or serves as an excuse to define women exclusively in terms of their sexual role is completely ruled out.

So what significance did Christianity have for the emancipation of women in the early church? The answer is that Christianity did not produce women's liberation, but it could have encouraged it and should have done more to do so than just through alternative forms of life. Instead of this, in the second and third centuries a shift took place: there was increasing hostility to women in the church teaching and practice of the following centuries. Since in the society of late antiquity women had largely already achieved their emancipation, 'the abundant prohibitions after the third century of women participating in church office attest contrary practices which become all the clearer, the more they are repeated': 'So the political and dogmatic growth of orthodoxy goes hand in hand with the battle against the emancipation of women in both church and society.'[34]

Things need not have turned out like this, since both the ancient humanist heritage and the message of the gospel could have pointed in another direction. But in respect of the present day it must be said that what may still have been 'understandable' for the Christianity of the Hellenistic paradigm of the early church becomes completely incomprehensible if open or latent discrimination against women in Christian churches is still grounded in and maintained with the support of 'church tradition'. So here too questions arise for the future. These questions must be put above all to the Orthodox and Roman Catholic churches.

But there is one thing that women, too, should never forget. The male domination which imperceptibly became established in the church of the Hellenistic paradigm and then even more in the mediaeval Roman Catholic paradigm would hardly have been conceivable in this form without a prohibition which does not appear anywhere in the New Testament: the prohibition of the marriage of the clergy (the law of celibacy). In the Eastern churches, of course, this applies only to bishops, but in the Roman Catholic church it was also imposed on all priests and deacons. As Peter Brown rightly says:

> At this point Christianity chose the 'great refusal'. In the very centuries when the rabbinate was achieving its paramount position because it accepted marriage as a quasi-obligatory criterion of wisdom, the leaders of the Christian community orientated themselves in a diametrically opposed direction. Access to leading positions in the Christian community is identified with a quasi-obligatory celibacy. Seldom has a power structure been built up with such speed and such a sharp drawing of boundaries, on the basis of so intimate an act as sexual renunciation.[35]

# 3 Women in the Church of the Middle Ages

In the West, after the fifth century a new mediaeval-Latin paradigm developed (P III), succeeding the original Jewish–Christian paradigm and the Hellenistic paradigm of the early church. It was made up of three elements, which had a negative effect on the position of women:

- the Latin theology of Augustine, which was different from the theology of the Greek church fathers;
- the formation of the Roman papacy as a central institution for ruling the church;
- the new kind of piety among the Germanic peoples.

## Augustine: original sin corrupts sexuality

Augustine's great achievement has often been praised, and needs no further emphasis. Indeed, it is impossible here to come anywhere near assessing his epoch-making work and all the wise and profound, brilliant and moving things he wrote about the human longing for happiness in the world, under the rule of sin and the rule of grace; all his deep thoughts on time and eternity, spirituality and piety, surrender to God and the human soul. But there can be no doubt that Augustine, who so impressively advocated the primacy of the will, of love, in the face of the Greek primacy of the intellect, and who ventured such a bold statement as *Dilige, et quod vis fac*, 'Love, and do what you will';[1] who could write in so grand a style on the grace of God, is also responsible for highly problematical developments in the Latin church, not only in the theology of grace, the sacraments and the Trinity, but also in sexual morality.

According to Augustine, human beings have been deeply corrupted right from the beginning by Adam's fall: 'in him all have sinned' (Rom. 5.12). What Augustine found in the Latin Bible translation of his time was *in quo*, and he referred this 'in him' to Adam. But the original Greek text simply has *eph'ho* = 'because' (or 'in that') all sinned! So what did Augustine read out of this sentence in Romans? Not only a primal sin of Adam but an inherited sin, original sin, which every human being has from birth. For Augustine, this was the reason why every human being, even the tiny infant, is poisoned in body and soul. All would incur eternal death unless they were baptized.

And worse still, because of his personal experience of the power of sex and his Manichaean past, Augustine – in contrast to Paul, who does not write a word about it – associates this transmission of 'original sin' with the sexual act and the fleshly (= selfish) desires, concupiscence, which are connected with it.[2] Indeed Augustine puts sexuality generally right at the centre of human nature.

Thus Augustine above all is responsible for the suppression of sexuality in Western theology and the Western church. More than other Latin theologians (e.g. Jerome), Augustine stressed the equality of man and woman at least on a spiritual level (in respect of their rational intelligence) because both are in the image of God. But at the same time he maintained the physical subordination of the woman which was general at the time – according to Genesis 2, the woman is created from the man and for the man.[3] In all this, Augustine's theory of sex and sin remains problematical.[4]

This is because for Augustine it was clear that ideally sexual intercourse should take place only for the procreation of children. Sexual pleasure purely for its own sake is sinful and to be suppressed; it was inconceivable for him that sexual pleasure could even enrich and deepen the relationship between husband and wife. This Augustinian legacy of the vilification of sexual libido represented a tremendous burden for the men and women of the Middle Ages, the Reformation, and long afterwards. And to think that in our own day a pope has proclaimed in all earnestness the view that even in marriage a husband can look on his wife 'unchastely', if he does so purely for pleasure!

## Rigorism in sexual morality

Original sin is transferred by sexual pleasure during intercourse. As was pointed out by the Catholic moral theologian Josef Georg Ziegler:

> The devastating effect of Augustine's association of original sin and sexual pleasure was that over the centuries it ruled out any open approach to marital intercourse and thus to marriage generally. Following the African church teachers, early scholastic theology put forward the view that original sin is transmitted by the sexual pleasure of the marital act.[5]

There is no mistaking the fact that in the face of increasingly marked moral degeneration as early as the Merovingian period, in the Carolingian period a sexual-moral rigorism established itself on a broad front, influenced by numerous primitive sexual taboos associated with sexual anxiety.[6] It governed not so much the official doctrine and penitential practice of the mediaeval church as unofficial teaching and practices.

For the clergy, who since Boniface's church reform had been required to observe sexual continence under threat of harsh penalties, this meant that anyone who wanted to come into contact with sacred things had to have 'pure', 'unsullied' hands (hence, even now, the anointing of hands at the ordination of priests). Sex, even if involuntary (emissions of semen) or permissible (in marriage), excluded them from encounter with the holy.

For the laity this meant that they were excluded from

preparation of and contact with the holy forms (hence no communion in the hands), indeed that women even had to be kept out of the sanctuary. Male semen, menstrual blood and blood lost in childbirth brought moral impurity and excluded those concerned from receiving the sacraments.

We need to reflect on the sexual repression that those countless penitentiaries with their often contradictory catalogues of sins or punishments created – all in the name of God and the church. 'Continence', in late antiquity the ideal of particular élites, was now as far as possible imposed on the whole population as an ideal. This morality, so hostile to pleasure, stipulated with merciless casuistry that

- during the days of their menstruation women were not to enter the church nor receive communion, and that after giving birth they needed a special blessing;
- the emission of seed, especially if it was caused deliberately, made men impure;
- married couples must refrain from sexual intercourse not only during menstruation and in the period before and after giving birth, but also on all Sundays and high feast days along with their vigils and octaves, on certain days of the week (Fridays), and in Advent and Lent. There is no doubt that the intention here was a rigorous limitation of marital sexual intercourse, and the giving of pleasure even in marriage was put in the background. For sexual stimulation was intrinsically bad, even if it was involuntary. Only in the course of the thirteenth century was at least the view of the sinfulness of any sense of pleasure overcome. But enough of a rigoristic pessimism about sex and marriage remained: sexual pleasure was legitimated only by other motives – principally the purpose of procreation.[7]

## An inter-religious problem

Here too – though one might hardly expect it – an inter-religious problem arises which also affects Judaism and Islam. We need to pause briefly over it here. Not least because of the Christian sexual morality of the Middle Ages, there has been talk of a 'Judaized Christianity', often as though this were a historical fact, often also in polemic. Is this right?

Granted, there is no disputing the fact that in particular the Christianity of the Carolingians, at whose court Charlemagne was celebrated as the new David, Moses or Joshua, and scholars often addressed one another with biblical names, had features reminiscent of the Old Testament. And it is also beyond dispute that the commandment to tithe, the sabbath (Sunday) rest and the instruction about unleavened bread occur in the Hebrew Bible but not in the New Testament, and that the Hebrew Bible also contains explicit regulations about sexual pollution and cultic impurity.

Nevertheless, it is wrong here simply to speak of Judaizing. For both in the Hebrew Bible and in the New Testament and the Qur'an we find two lines of ideas and attitudes:

- Both the Hebrew Bible and the New Testament and the Qur'an affirm sexuality and human love as intrinsically the gift of the Creator: man and woman are created for each other in their bodily nature as well, and are to become 'one flesh'.
- Not only the Hebrew Bible but also the New Testament and the Qur'an contain certain restrictions on sexual intercourse. For example, the Qur'an, too, forbids it during the wife's menstruation, during the day in times of fasting and also during the pilgrimage to Mecca. And even though no such restrictions are prescribed in the New Testament (in any case, some were assumed as a matter of course against the Jewish background), here in particular

(in contrast to the Hebrew Bible and the Qur'an) celibacy
is praised by Paul, even if it is nowhere required.

In our time, cultural anthropologists have been able to
demonstrate the degree to which sexual customs and modes of
expression have become norms and patterns of orientation
required by a culture. They have shown how notions that the
emission of seed and menstrual blood are intrinsically defiling
are not specifically Jewish but widespread in archaic pre-
ethical thought. Some of them are also part of ancient natural
medicine, and thus not specifically Jewish, Christian or Islamic.
And nowadays, isn't the question posed to all the religions of
Near Eastern origin this: should, can, the present-day view of
sexuality in religion still proceed from notions and attitudes
which involve an archaic understanding of human beings and
God? Or from an ancient natural medicine which, for example,
has the erroneous view that blood lost in menstruation and in
giving birth is a poisonous emission, and that sexual intercourse during pregnancy damages the child? A cultic sexual
purity has for·all too long been advocated for clergy and laity. In
contrast to Judaism and Islam, in Christianity a depreciation of
sexuality and marriage has been encouraged by the high esteem
associated with a religiously motivated celibacy. The Roman
church also played a leading role here.

## A church of celibate men and the prohibition of marriage

In the Latin paradigm of the Middle Ages the Roman church
was now increasingly to take on a profile of its own, so that this
Catholic paradigm will present itself in its consummate form as
a Roman Catholic paradigm. But it was a long way from Pope
Damasus, the self-confident contemporary of Augustine, to
Pope Gregory VII in the eleventh century. Gregory VII established the Roman view in the Catholic church and the German
empire in a life and death fight with the German emperor, even

if he personally came to grief. This in principle laid not only a theological foundation (that of Augustine) but also a church-political foundation for a new paradigm of the church: the paradigm of a Catholic church centred on Rome.

The Roman system brought to the Catholic church of the West centralization (an absolutist papal church), legalization (a church with canon law), politicization (a powerful church) and militarization (a militant church). None of these had been customary previously. Above all, it also brought clericalization. Under the influence of the monks and Hildebrand, who was later to become Pope Gregory VII, in a kind of 'pan-monasticism' Rome required unconditional obedience, the renunciation of marriage and communal life for all the clergy. The resolutions of the Lateran Synod of 1059 on the prohibition of priestly marriage were followed more in France, the cradle of monastic reform, than in Italy. At any rate the prohibition against priestly marriage was not proclaimed by the bishops of Lombardy – except by the Bishop of Brescia, who was almost beaten to death by his priests for doing so. But this perseverance of the clergy in legitimate priestly marriage led to another revolt of the powerful movement of the Patareni (from *pattari*, 'old clothes dealers', 'scrap dealers') against them, again encouraged by the pope. There were repulsive drives against wives of priests in the clergy houses.

The indignation over the prohibition of marriage was even greater in Germany than in Italy. There only three bishops (those of Salzburg, Würzburg and Passau) dared to proclaim the Roman decrees, one of them (the last) at Christmas: he was driven out and almost lynched by the clergy. The lesser clergy were particularly affected by the condemnation, and they protested in their thousands (3600 clergy at a synod in the diocese of Constance alone) against the new laws and the stirring up of the church people against their spiritual leaders. In a petition the German clergy made the following case:

1.  Did the pope not know the word of the Lord, 'He who is able to receive it, let him receive it' (Matt. 19.12)?
2.  The pope was compelling men by force to live as angels; he wanted to forbid the course of nature. This would only lead to unchastity.
3.  Faced with the choice whether to give up the priestly office or marriage, they would decide for marriage. Let the pope recruit angels for the ministry of the church.[8]

Here again it was Gregory VII who introduced the definitive decision by accepting the petitions of the Patareni and endorsing the resolutions of 1059 at his first Lenten synod in 1074. Indeed, he suspended all the married priests (who were censured as 'concubinarians') and at the same time mobilized the laity not to accept any priestly functions from them. This was new: a boycott of the clergy by the laity staged by the pope himself.

However, the Second Lateran Council of 1139 was the first to draw conclusions for church law by declaring consecration to higher orders (from the sub-diaconate upwards) to be a hindrance to marriage. This meant that priestly marriage which, while forbidden, had been legally valid, was now a priori invalid. All wives of priests were regarded as concubines; indeed, the children of priests were made the property of the church, slaves. So from now on there was a universal and compulsory law of celibacy, though in practice it was only observed to a limited degree up to the Reformation, even in Rome.

More than anything else, the mediaeval, typically Roman Catholic law of celibacy – over which there is again much dispute today – contributed to the elevation of the 'clergy' , the 'hierarchy'. The 'priestly state' was removed from the 'people' (who became the 'laity') and set completely above it; now the state of celibacy was beyond dispute regarded as morally more 'perfect' than that of marriage. Indeed clericalization was now so extensive that the 'church' and the 'clergy' were virtually identified – terminology which has lasted to the present day. For the exercise of power, this meant:

- The laity were excluded from the church, which hitherto had consisted of clergy and laity.
- As those who administered the means of grace, the clergy alone formed 'the church'.
- The church of the clergy had a hierarchical and monarchical organization with the pope at its head, so that Ecclesia Catholica and Ecclesia Romana became synonymous.
- The clergy ('church') and laity formed 'Christendom' (*Christianitas*), but in it, according to the Roman view, pope and clergy had to dominate.

Now in the high Middle Ages the clergy consisted more than ever of two powerful branches: the secular clergy and the clergy in religious orders. And it was in the time of Innocent III in particular that the significance of the clergy in religious orders was decisively to increase. Not only were the monks in the West now increasingly priests (*patres*), with lay brothers (*fratres*) only for more menial services. It was Innocent III in particular who wisely domesticated the poverty movement in the church and approved those novel orders in which discipleship of the poor Jesus was the leading idea: the mendicant orders of the Franciscans and Dominicans, as we shall see in more detail.

Over clericalization, too, a striking difference between the early Byzantine church (P II) and the mediaeval Roman Catholic paradigm (P III) is evident:

- In the Eastern churches the clergy, apart from the bishops, remained married and therefore seemed very much closer to the people and more assimilated to the structure of society.
- But the celibate clergy of the West seemed totally removed from the Christian people, above all because they were

unmarried. They had their own, dominant social status, totally superior to the lay state and totally subordinate to the Roman pope, who was now for the first time supported by an omnipresent, centrally organized, available and mobile celibate troop of auxiliaries: the mendicant orders. The most significant theologian among them was the Dominican Thomas Aquinas.

## Thomas: women – somewhat defective

The brilliant man from Aquino, who only very much later was to become the *Doctor communis*, the 'universal teacher' of Roman Catholic Christianity, created the classical mediaeval synthesis. By comparison with his great predecessor Augustine, Thomas favours reason over faith, nature over grace, philosophy over theology, and the human over what is distinctively Christian. All this, which has often been appraised, can again only be touched on here.

By way of excuse, it has been said that for all his universality, Thomas did not understand three things: art, children and women. Because of his monastic and celibate way of life that is at least understandable in the case of women. But didn't he say quite basic and historically influential things about women and their nature? Defenders of Thomas point out that he only dealt with women here and there throughout his work, as it were incidentally. But at two crucial points in the *Summa theologiae* there are quite basic statements about women: within the doctrine of creation a whole *quaestio* with four articles on the 'bringing forth' (*productio*) of the woman (from Adam),[9] and within the framework of the doctrine of grace an important article on the right of women to speak in church.[10]

Now it must be said straight away that for Thomas Aquinas there was no doubt:

- that woman, like man, is created in the image of God;
- that woman therefore in principle has the same dignity and the same eternal destiny for her soul as man;
- that woman *was created by God not only for procreation but also for a shared life.*

So Thomas Aquinas may not simply be depicted as a dark mediaeval misogynist. But is that a reason for playing down his other statements? In matters relating to the 'theology of the feminine', didn't Thomas accentuate and refine many of Augustine's remarks and as a result not diminish but intensify the contempt for women? Didn't he assert with reference to the biblical account of creation that man is the 'starting point and goal of woman', and that there is something deficient and unsuccessful (*aliquid deficiens et occasionatum*) about woman?[11] Didn't he say that a woman is a man who by chance is defective and unsuccessful, a *mas occasionatus*?[12] This remark of Thomas has been much quoted.

Given this finding from the doctrine of creation, do we need to look far for explanations as to why women have absolutely no say at all in the mediaeval church? Granted, in the light of the Old Testament they could not in principle be denied the gift of prophecy. But what about the ordination of women as priests? While Thomas was unable to discuss this in more detail in the *Summa*, since he broke off working on it, in his younger days he had come to a negative conclusion on this question in his *Commentary on the Sentences*.[13] Here he asserts not only the illegitimacy but even the invalidity of such an ordination. Moreover this view was promptly taken up in the posthumous supplements to the *Summa* (*Supplementum*) as Thomas' valid position.[14] The same applies to women's preaching.[15]

But anyone who on the basis of all these negative statements immediately wants to pass a definitive, negative, judgment on Thomas should remember three things. First, Thomas is anything but original in many of his remarks; rather, in many cases he is simply expressing what people (men) thought at that time. Secondly, in some of his statements Thomas is simply basing himself on the Bible, on the Old Testament (for example, women inherit only when there are no male descendants; men must not wear women's clothes) or even the New Testament (for example, woman are created for the sake of man, women are to keep silent in church). Thirdly, as a 'progressive theologian', for his knowledge of women Thomas followed the greatest scientific and philosophical authority of his time, to whom there was hardly any alternative: Aristotle. And it was Aristotle who in his treatise *On the Procreation of Living Beings* provided the biological basis for a fatal 'sexual metaphysics' and 'theology of the sexes'.

For already according to Aristotle a woman is a 'failed man'. Why? Applying his theory of act/form and potency/matter to physiology, Aristotle asserts that in the procreation of a new human being the male is the sole active, 'procreative' part by virtue of his sperm (the *virtus activa*). By contrast, the woman is the exclusively receptive, passive part, the receptive matter which merely makes available the disposition (*virtus passiva*) for the new person. Thomas, too, asserts just this, and also follows Aristotle in meeting the difficulty why it is that in one case a male fathers a boy and in another case a girl. This can be due to a weakness in the male procreative power, to the female disposition, or to an external influence: the north wind for a boy and the (moist) south wind for a girl, so that in one case a full man and in the other only a 'failed' man is born. We can imagine the devastating effect that for centuries such views had. For it was only in 1827 that the existence of a female ovum was demonstrated, and it took even longer to discover the precise way in which ovum and spermatozoa come together in procreation. None of this is any excuse (Galen, the most famous doctor of Roman antiquity, had assumed an active biological role of the woman in the production of the foetus), but it does explain some things.

Nevertheless, for the sake of historical justice it must be added that in the face of the prevailing Augustinianism Thomas Aquinas contributed more than others of his time to a universal philosophical and theological revaluation of the material reality of creation (corporeality) and was more positive about sexuality than his teacher Augustine. However, that does not fundamentally alter the anthropology of Augustine and Thomas, which the Norwegian Catholic historian of theology Kari Børresen has investigated thoroughly in various fundamental works.[16] Her conclusion is that both Augustine and Thomas without any doubt advocate an androcentric anthropology centred on the man. Both regard the theory of the relationship between the man and the woman not from the perspective of a reciprocal relationship but from the perspective of the male. The male is seen as the exemplary sex, and the nature and role of the woman are understood in terms of him. So there is hierarchical superiority and subordination instead of reciprocal complementarity. Thomas corrected Augustine in different ways without explicitly adopting a standpoint opposing him.[17]

## Women in the family, politics and business

Even more than in other eras, research into women in the Middle Ages is in flux, driven on by feminist scholars who are convinced that above all in the churches the self-understanding and behaviour patterns of women today are still under the influence of the Middle Ages. At that time, it is thought, even when women were praised, the patriarchal culture caused them to be measured by male criteria ('the weaker sex'!). However, it is proving easier for feminist research to reconstruct mediaeval theories, discourses and models than to rediscover how women really lived.[18]

Now we have indeed discovered the reasons[19] why despite all the beginnings made in antiquity and early Christianity women were prevented from having truly equal status even in the early church. They include the establishment of hierarchical structures and male domination specifically in the sacramental sphere; a hostility to sexuality which was typical of the time even outside the monasteries, in church and society; and finally the disparagement of education, which for women in particular was sometimes openly scorned. And we have similarly seen[20] how later, in the Carolingian period, a rigoristic sexual morality, both for the clergy (the prohibition of marriage) and for the laity (the prohibition of touching the sacred forms and the exclusion of women even from the sanctuary), broke through on a broad front. Nor should we forget the pernicious influence of the penitentials disseminated on the continent of Europe by Irish-Scottish and Anglo-Saxon monks, which attempted to repress sexual intercourse. What is a 'mediaeval world'? In the ideal view of the church it was a world governed by priests, monks, nuns and their ideal of continence. These figures were not just the only vehicles of a written education, but they also occupied the highest rank on the Christian scale, because they already embodied the kingdom of heaven even now, without marriage and (private) property.

However, for the married this meant that precisely because the body was now regarded as a sacrosanct temple, it might only be united with a body of the other sex, if at all, if this union took place for the purpose of procreation. Contraception was therefore put on the same level as abortion and the exposure of children. So we can understand how Jacques LeGoff can speak of a great 'cultural revolution' (I would call it a paradigm shift) involving the body: after antiquity, which with its theatres, baths, stadia and arenas was so positive about the body, there was now a Middle Ages which despised the body (and especially the female body) as a prison of the soul, because it was the seat of sexuality and the 'infection of the flesh' by original sin. Here 'a doctrinal derailment of the bodily'[21] became evident. All in all, this was a defeat for the body and women's bodies in particular, since these bodies were seen as being particularly prone to the temptations of Satan. Here we have the beginnings of the witch-craze.

At the end of antiquity, when at least upper-class women had great opportunities, Roman law and culture still gave them some freedom. However, we might ask, didn't a free Germanic woman originally also have a greater degree of personal self-determination, sexual freedom, economic independence and the right to consent to marriage than has long been assumed? There is a discussion about this in contemporary feminist scholarship in connection with the early Middle Ages. This research is rewarding in providing a picture of how women really lived.[22]

For feminist scholars today are no longer content with the well-known fact that women could play a by no means insignificant role as rulers: women like Adelheid, Theophanu, Agnes or Constance, and also abbesses (e.g. Mathilde of Quedlinburg, the sister of Otto II) and other women of the aristocratic upper class already among the Merovingians, the Carolingians and the Ottonians. This was especially true of the 'first lady' of the empire (*consors imperii*), whose position was a notable one, from the coronation liturgy to *de facto* regency or (if there were no descendants) even sole regency. Statues from the early Middle Ages portray king and queen side by side on equal terms. Even in the second half of the twelfth century the women in aristocratic lay society were usually more educated than their husbands, who were usually illiterate (as was the Emperor Frederick Barbarossa). In France and Italy, too, these aristocratic women could always exercise considerable *de facto* political influence (but not constitutionally), in particular in widowhood: we may recall the widowed Margrave Mathilda of Tuscany, the mistress of Canossa, who was an indispensable ally to Gregory VII in his historic struggle. Women could administer dowries and possessions inherited from their husbands and freely decide to remarry.

But what does all this say about the social status and self-understanding of the mass of women at this time? Not very much. That noblewomen could in some cases become as significant as noblemen is merely the exception which proves the rule. For there is no overlooking the fact that even in the high Middle Ages the social structure continued to have an utterly patriarchal stamp. Granted, the fact that slavery had been abolished at least since the time of the Carolingians and had been transformed into 'serfdom' had a positive effect. But in the Christian Mediterranean, and especially in ports like Genoa, there were still countless slaves (male and female, not least from Muslim countries). As to the degree that women in the Middle Ages were free at all and not slaves or serfs, they were usually neither capable of holding a fief, nor could they swear an oath before a court, so they were not regarded as eligible for military service.

In the family and the home the will of the master of the house prevailed. Certainly women had their share of civic freedoms. But these were not personal freedoms in the modern sense; they were the corporate freedom of the middle class, the civic community, guilds and other corporations. And certainly the fully developed city offered women more possibilities than before, in crafts, retail and on occasion even wholesale trade. But we need to note that it did not offer them the same rights and the same rewards, nor did it offer them any political say – unless they belonged to a small class of regents and noblewomen.

If we follow the study by the Bonn mediaevalist Edith Ennen of women in the Middle Ages for the area between the Seine and the Rhine, that second focal point in the development of mediaeval cities alongside the cities of upper Italy, we find 'that the woman had only a passive share in the great development of urban life in the twelfth and thirteenth centuries, as the consort and helper of the man'.[23] Specifically, that means:

> She was not one of the jurors in the cities of northern France, nor did she sit on the city councils which formed as urban organs in thirteenth-century German cities. She shared the risk of the serf, the small man who went to the city and started a new life there with the money that he had raised by selling his property or simply with his own labour. She contributed to her social rise, as far as the profits of a city merchant allowed her, by wearing valuable clothes, having maids, and living in and running a large and well-equipped house. Probably she already worked professionally in city trade. But we know little of that before 1250.[24]

Of course circumstances varied greatly, depending on time and place. And anyone who does not look for just one cause in passing judgment will concede that there were several reasons for the gender-specific division of work which resulted in a stereotyping of the roles of the sexes to the detriment of women:

- the increase in the population since the seventh century, possibly favoured by a warming of the climate between the tenth and twelfth centuries (a surplus of women is disputed);
- the development of new techniques, like the heavy plough which went deeper and the use of horses which were shod and harnessed;
- the redevelopment of the Roman cities in the West, which had contracted since the fifth and sixth centuries, and the marked influx from the country;
- the rise of a middle class with legal (not social) equality and free from the control of the lord of the city (who was usually a bishop);
- the development of an urban, mercantile, business market economy which deprived agriculture of its previous significance as the means of securing survival. On the whole though, the crafts and trades were men's work, and the household was a household of women;

- the university and thus all the academic professions continued to be closed to women for centuries; the (male) scholars educated at the universities penetrated the governments of country and city and were now indispensable as doctors, notaries and procurators. This forced women into merely auxiliary posts because they lacked academic training. For example, women could not become professional doctors, but could become assistants, nurses, midwives.

As the historian Annette Kuhn reports, much research into women in the Middle Ages revolves around the 'central question of the conditions and the reasons for the exclusion of women from the development of the capitalist economy'.[25] Following the American historian Martha Howell,[26] Kuhn distinguishes two interconnected but different systems which cross in women's work: the first system describes a 'sphere of work in which the woman works in her own capacity as mother, sexual partner, creditor, guarantor of subsistence (food and clothing) and for the market'. But a second system crosses with this: 'the economy in the sense of an economic movement starting from the capitalist market which among other things also leads to a hierarchy of work and an unequal evaluation of work, e.g. as productive and less productive work'.[27] Certain contradictions in women's lives can be explained from this duality of traditional household economy and the new mercantile capitalism. But so much for economics. What about the church?

### Repression of women in the church

The church, too, presents a deeply ambivalent picture. Certainly it must be recognized that through its theology and practice of marriage the church contributed to the revaluation of woman in society. Thus in the twelfth century the church established that the mutual declaration of intent, in other words the consent of the partners, was an essential part of a marriage, and this presupposed their fundamental equality.[28] The church also saw to it that – contrary to a persistent abuse in the form of clandestine (secret) marriages – marriage was formally concluded in public. Indeed at this time, when the doctrine of the seven sacraments was developed, above all by Peter Lombard and Thomas Aquinas, marriage was given the status of one of the seven sacraments: this was the foundation for the indissolubility of marriage and strengthened the self-confidence of women.

On the other hand, the same church, in which the pope appeared as the 'father' and the 'church' (hierarchy) as the 'mother' of Christianity, in which celibacy was forced on the secular clergy and the codification of church law took on dramatic proportions, encouraged an intensified patriarchalization of the power structures and norms. Now there was a repression of women (in part also legal) which has remained a characteristic of the Roman Catholic paradigm to the present day. A symptom of this at the time was that the ruler's wife now had to be at a due distance behind her consort, accompanied by her ladies in waiting. The abbesses, who also had spiritual authority, were restricted to their jurisdictional authority. With an argument from the Old Testament, the law of inheritance was limited to the male (patrilinear) succession (unless male descendants were lacking). But even more important:

- Canon law (already the *Decretum Gratiani*) prescribed that women were subject to men with an argument from natural law.
- The church's ideal for women's existence was primarily the nun, who leads a continent life, well pleasing to God, free of earthly ties. Yet the lay culture and court poetry which arose in the twelfth century already shows a new secular ideal for women which was expressed by the

Minnesingers, who were not only men but women (the existence of the latter is often overlooked), and was to be developed further in the Italian Renaissance.

• Women remained excluded from all church offices, and were even repeatedly forbidden to preach because of the attractiveness of the Cathars and Waldensians, with their positive attitude towards women.

The Waldensian movement, with its ideal of poverty, which formed around the merchant Petrus Waldes in Lyons around 1170–80, wanted to restore the Christian faith to its original purity, going back to the form of life adopted by the disciples of Jesus, men and women. For this lay movement within the church it was a matter of course that women should engage in public preaching with equal rights: this was a particular thorn in the flesh of the church hierarchy. The Waldensians were excommunicated in 1184/85, and in 1215 were finally condemned as 'heretics' at the Fourth Lateran Council.[29]

Unfortunately things were no better in the religious orders. Some monastic orders even opposed parallel foundations for women. The new religious communities of women which came into being in the spirit of Dominic and Francis (sometimes at the request of the women themselves and mostly by papal decree) were finally put under the corresponding male orders to integrate them into the established forms of church religious life. Other communities 'of virgins and widows dedicated to God', living in the world, which first formed in the Netherlands for religious and economic reasons and worked for a living in craft and charitable activity, were even declared heretical. Their name, 'Beguines', may be a truncated form of 'Albigensians', i.e. heretics (these were suppressed by the Council of Vienne in 1311). Here again we have a history of church persecutions which also affected the parallel male communities, the Beghards.[30]

Here, too, we certainly must not overlook the fact that within the sphere of the church at that time women had space and possibilities of influence which society did not offer them. There was space for unmarried women and widows who in their attachment to religious orders and the church found a safe, fulfilled existence, with new possibilities of education and influence and a new female self-confidence, Here, too, Edith Ennen may be right: 'In the new dawn of the twelfth and thirteenth centuries women thronged into the convents of their own free will purely to become disciples of Christ.'[31] That nobility often used the convents as welfare institutions for daughters and widows is less important here than that the womenfolk of well-to-do parents received a basic education in reading, writing and doctrine in the cities, even outside the convents; however, only in exceptional cases could they get a specialist education.

But this thronging into the convents must not be confused with a movement which brought women political freedom. It derived from an interest in piety which was increasingly also taking hold of the grass roots, an interest which moved over into the world of women from the mediaeval male world of the Benedictines, Cistercians and Premonstratensians, and finally the Franciscans and Dominicans, However, we should note that in the early Middle Ages the convents were virtually only for women from the aristocracy. And how deeply this class thinking was rooted is shown by the most important woman religious of the time, Hildegard of Bingen (1098–1179).[32] Even in the twelfth century she wanted to maintain the privilege of the nobility, although leading monasteries like Cluny, Hirsau and later Cîteaux had long since given up the privileges of birth. However, such class-specific separation could not be maintained any longer. For now an increasing number of urban patricians, daughters or wives of estate officials and citizens, were entering convents in order to attain perfection in keeping with the gospel and certainly also to attain economic and social security and independence outside marriage. Still, for women from the middle and lower classes at this time it was sometimes difficult to get a place in a convent – either because the convents were full or because the women had no dowry.

Women religious were only rarely active in church politics: outstanding examples like Hildegard of Bingen, Birgitta of Sweden, Catherine of Siena and later Teresa of Avila are only the exceptions which again prove the rule. But there was one area in the high and late Middle Ages – apart from poetry (Hroswith of Gandersheim) and crafts (weaving, embroidery) – in which women were not only men's equals but often showed more imagination and creativity: mysticism. Hildegard of Bingen was already a versatile writer and visionary mystic. And she not only published mystical books interpreting the world – that famous book *Scivias*, or 'Know the Ways' – but also composed works on nature and medicine which today are the most important sources for the knowledge of nature in Central Europe in the early Middle Ages. She composed 70 spiritual songs and undertook three great preaching journeys; she was a unique woman, in whom spirituality and empirical sensitivity, wide-ranging interests and mystical depths were combined. Mysticism – let's look at that more closely.

## Mysticism under suspicion

Beyond question, women played a quite special role in German mysticism,[33] the significance of which has often been suppressed by men like Meister Eckhart, Johann Tauler, Heinrich Suso and Jan van Ruysbroeck. But like the Benedictine convent at Bingen by the Rhine under Abbess Hildegard in the twelfth century, in the thirteenth century the Cistercian convent of Helfta (close to Eisleben, later the place of Luther's birth and death), which was regarded as the 'crown of German convents', was an important centre of mysticism. It was here that Gertrude of Hackeborn, who was elected abbess at the age of 19 and was to lead the convent for 41 years, was active, and here too lived a young sister who also had mystical gifts, Mechthild of Hackeborn. Gertrude of Helfta (later called 'the Great') was also accepted into the convent at an early age. The convent was also the scene of the activity of Mechthild of Magdeburg, who had already become famous as a mystic with her six books of the 'Flowing Light of the Godhead'. Living as a Beguine in accordance with the rule of Dominic, Mechthild had made enemies in the Dominican order in particular as a result of her reports of mystical experiences (for the first time in German!) and her criticism of the religious and secular clergy. She had every reason to complain bitterly about injustices and calumnies and finally to enter the convent of Helfta.

So is it entirely surprising that wherever mysticism in Christianity threatened to be the main thing instead of an enrichment, it came up against resistance? Moreover, conflicts with the official Roman Catholic Church, which feared the loss of its monopoly of the communication of word and sacrament, shadow the rise of mysticism. But why here (P III), in contrast to the East (P II), was there always repression and excommunication? The translator of the works of Pseudo-Dionysius, John Scotus Eriugena, was condemned by a council in Valence in 855 for his views of predestination. The writings of the mystics, men and women, were constantly suspect; indeed, many great mystics like Meister Eckhart, Teresa of Avila, John of the Cross and Madame Guyon (and her protector Fénélon) were pursued by the Inquisition. And that Beguine, the mystic Marguerite Porete, who around 1300 had written the *Miroir des simples âmes* ('Mirror of simple souls'), was not just condemned as a heretic by the Bishop of Cambrai in 1306. Marguerite, whose work lived on after her condemnation in four languages and six versions, but anonymously, and apparently had an important influence on Meister Eckhart,[34] was again accused in 1308, transported to Paris, interrogated by the Inquisition (here she refused to say anything about her teaching) and was finally burnt at the stake in 1310.[35]

However, it has to be pointed out that while a mystical attitude of prayer can be important for Christians, it cannot claim to be the norm, as if mystical immersion were the highest form of prayer. So for all the admiration for the great Teresa of Avila, that brilliant woman who is one of the most significant mystics in the history of religion, in neither the Old nor the New Testament is there any ideal of an inner prayer or a prayer of the heart; there is no invitation to observe, describe and analyse mystical experiences and states. No stepladder of mystical prayer leading to ecstasy can be recognized, and there is no emphasis on any prayer which presupposes a special religious gift. Mystical prayer is a charism, just one charism among others, and not the highest. It can serve a discipleship of Christ which culminates in love, but it can also – if it becomes an end in itself – lead away from it.

As we saw, mediaeval piety is unthinkable without mysticism, especially women's mysticism, although this mysticism could never become paradigmatic for theology and the church. But mediaeval piety is also unthinkable without the growth of Marian piety, in which the paradigm shift can once again be demonstrated vividly – to some degree in the micro-sphere.

## Veneration of Mary on the increase

Here we must note in advance that much as veneration of Mary increased in the Latin high Middle Ages, not only in church customs, in church festivals and ceremonies, but also in poetry and art, it must nevertheless be recognized that veneration of Mary first developed in the Hellenistic Byzantine paradigm (P II).[36]

For in the East there was an age-old tradition of the cult of mother deities, particularly in Asia Minor, which could be fruitfully used for veneration of Mary: in the form of a cult of the 'perpetual virgin', the 'mother of God' and exalted 'queen of heaven'. It was in the East that Mary was first invoked in prayer ('Under Your Protection', third/fourth centuries), and the commemoration of Mary was introduced into the liturgy. It was in the East that legends about Mary were first told and hymns to Mary composed; churches were first named after Mary, Marian feasts introduced and images of Mary created.

The dogmatic statements about Mary can only be explained against this background. For only a council in the East could arrive at the idea of committing the church to belief in Mary as 'Mother of God', namely the Council of Ephesus in 431. We know now that this momentous christological statement particularly corresponded to the political interests of a man who knew the grandstand ploys with which to manipulate this council: Cyril of Alexandria. Even before the arrival of the other party in the council from Antioch, which had spoken of Mary as 'Mother of Christ (*christotokos*), he had succeeded in carrying through his definition, 'Mother of God' (*theotokos*).[37] This was a new title, remote from the Bible, which was to provoke formulae even more open to misunderstanding.

So only in the East, in Ephesus, had it been possible to establish such a mariology, in a city whose inhabitants in any case worshipped the 'Great Mother' (originally the virgin goddess Artemis, Diana) and accordingly welcomed the substitute 'goddess' Mary with enthusiasm. The theological price paid for this did little to disturb such enthusiasm: the fact that the formula 'Mother of God' was suspect of Monophysitism (which was then corrected by Chalcedon) and led to a reification of the understanding of the divine Sonship and the incarnation. As if 'God' could be born, rather than a human being who as God's 'Son' is God's revelation for believers! This talk of a 'Mother of God' is partly responsible for the Jewish mistrust of Christianity even now and the present misunderstanding of many Muslims that the Christian Trinity is a triad consisting of God (father), Mary (mother) and Jesus (child).

By contrast, in the West, Eastern forms of piety connected with Mary did not become established without resistance. For example, in Augustine, at any rate, the theological father of the Latin mediaeval paradigm (P III), we find neither hymns nor prayers to Mary; not even feasts of Mary are mentioned. That is striking. Only in the fifth century do we find the first example of Mary being addressed in a Latin hymn ('*Salve sancta parens*', Caelius Sedulius). From this an increasingly rich Latin and later also Germanic body of poetry to Mary developed in the late sixth century.[38] Rome, too, now followed: in the sixth century Mary's name (and the title *Mater Dei*) was incorporated into the text of the mass; in the seventh century the Eastern feasts of Mary (Annunciation, Visitation, Birth, Purification) were introduced; towards the end of the tenth century legends were in circulation about the miraculous power of prayer to Mary.

Beyond doubt the climax of the mediaeval cult of Mary came in the eleventh/twelfth century. It is inconceivable without the influence of the Cistercian monk Bernard of Clairvaux. In the meantime the theological accents had increasingly shifted. It was no longer the role and activity of Mary the earthly mother of Jesus as depicted in the New Testament that now stood in the foreground. What was now decisive was Mary's cosmic role as the virgin mother of God and queen of heaven. Coupled with this was a process of idealization and exaltation. Whereas earlier church fathers still had spoken without hesitation about moral faults in Mary, now a perfect sinlessness of Mary was increasingly asserted, indeed a holiness even before her birth.

It was only logical that from the twelfth century on there were even individual voices which explicitly asserted that Mary had been preserved from original sin – which since Augustine had now become something like a basic dogma of the Catholic Church. It is true that at first such an exception to the fate of all humankind could not be established because of the opposition of the theologians, and especially of Thomas Aquinas. But this did not prevent the significant Franciscan theologian Duns Scotus (1308) later from seeking a 'speculative solution' and arguing: how can one maintain the dogma of the universality of original sin and at the same time declare Mary the exception? So Scotus invented the term 'anticipatory redemption' (*redemptio praeservativa*) of Mary – a purely theological construction. But now it was even harder to stop the process of the exaltation of Mary. Formally, distinctions were still maintained and were made between the general veneration of saints (*doulia*), heightened veneration of Mary (*hyperdoulia*) and worship of God (*latria*). But in practice Mary's creatureliness and humanity often played only a slight role.

However, the Mary of doctrine was one thing; the Mary of piety was another. In popular piety Mary, like Jesus himself – not least under the influence of Bernard and especially Francis of Assisi – took on more markedly human features. Mary appears in many prayers, hymns, songs and in many pictures and statues as the embodiment of mercy, as the intercessor who can obtain virtually anything from her heavenly son, as a loveable figure who stands nearer to human cares than the ascended and exalted divine Christ. Gothic style created an impressive 'cloaked Madonna' for this piety. This Madonna expresses in a unique way what millions of people often felt about Mary: she is the helper particularly of ordinary people, the oppressed, the anxious and the marginalized. A piece of mariology 'from below' becomes visible here, which contrasts with the dogmatic super-theories of 'Mary' among theologians, monks and hierarchs. This also explains the popularity of the biblical 'Ave Maria' from the twelfth century on; together with the 'Our Father' it became the most widespread form of prayer, though only since 1500 has it been prayed in its present form with a petition for support in the hour of death. It also explains the popularity of the 'Angelus', rung three times a day since the thirteenth century, and the prayer of the rosary, which has been practised since around the end of the thirteenth century.

## An ecumenical image of Mary?

The church in the Middle Ages guarded against just one thing: proclaiming any new Marian dogmas. This was reserved for the popes of the nineteenth and twentieth centuries, Pius IX and Pius XII. Pius IX in particular burdened the church with two dogmas at the same time by his policy. First he formally elevated to dogma, without any biblical foundation, Mary's Immaculate Conception (preservation from original sin). Then, sixteen years later, in his counter-revolutionary conservatism which was so opposed to the Enlightenment, science, democracy and freedom of religion, with the help of the First Vatican Council (1870) he also forced on the whole church the primacy and infallibility of the pope. Pius XII continued this line after the Second World War. Unconcerned in his Roman triumphalism about Protestant and Orthodox reservations and reservations within Catholicism, he had the ambition also to promulgate as a dogma Mary's bodily assumption to heavenly glory. He did this in 1950 as the climax of a 'Marian Age' which he himself then proclaimed.[39] Numerous appearances of Mary which 'took place', hardly by chance, in the nineteenth and early twentieth centuries (Lourdes, 1858 and Fatima, 1917) also fit in with this 'Marian climate'.

Thus what was not yet so clear in the Middle Ages was plainly demonstrated by the Pius Popes: here, and only here, papalism and Marianism go hand in hand as typical of the Roman Catholic paradigm. The background is doubtless celibacy which – as we heard – is deeply rooted in the mediaeval world. In the face of this development, the leading Catholic professor of feminist theology in Europe, the Dutchwoman Catharina Halkes, asks doubtfully: 'Is Mary a possible model which was exploited against women, which was not critical of men and which was to legitimate the gulf that the church had left open between (female) sexuality and the mediation of the saints?'[40] Beyond question a mediaeval Roman Catholic hierarchy which has remained mediaeval down to the twentieth century (with a pope like John Paul II, who has replaced the cross in the middle of his coat of arms with an M), which propagates celibacy for the clergy even in the face of thousands of parishes without pastors, and wants to tie sexual pleasure in the sphere of marriage to the procreation of children, created in the form of Mary a compensatory figure for unmarried clergy with whom in a 'spiritual way' one could experience intimacy, kindness, femininity and motherliness. Eugen Drewermann has described and analysed, with many examples, the fatal psychological consequences that this policy can and does have.[41]

It is also important to reflect on the effect of this Roman Catholic Marianism on the ecumenical movement within Christianity. Thus the Protestant theologian Jürgen Moltmann rightly points out:

> We have to note honestly and soberly that so far mariology has been more against ecumenism than for it. Mariology, as it has been developed further and further, has alienated Christians from Jews, the church from the New Testament, Protestant Christians from Catholic Christians and Christians generally from modern men and women. But is the Madonna of the church's mariology identical with Miriam, the Jewish mother of Jesus? Can we find the one in the other? Given the splits and separations which have been perpetrated in the name of the Madonna of the churches, should we not ask about the Jewish mother Miriam herself?[42]

Indeed, given this development in the framework of the mediaeval paradigm, it is appropriate to pause to reflect on what might be the future for the church. The figure of Mary needs to be liberated from certain images – from both the fantasies of a male celibate priestly hierarchy and the fantasies of women engaged in a compensatory search for identification. There can be no question here of spiriting away, indeed of destroying, the significance of Mary for theology, the church and the history of piety. Rather, the figure of Mary must be interpreted for our time in terms of her origins and liberated from so many misogynistic clichés and paralysing stereotypes. The aim must be to make the way free for a truly ecumenical image of Mary, so that the saying in Luke, 'Behold, from henceforth all generations shall call me blessed', can again hold in all the Christian churches.[43] There is still a dispute among feminists as to whether Mary can be an inspiring figure with whom they can identify. But at all events the following guidelines for an ecumenical picture of Mary seem to me to be important.

- According to the New Testament Mary is an utterly human being and not a heavenly being. The picture of Mary in the New Testament is extremely matter-of-fact and in part also contradictory. The earliest evangelist tells us only of a conflict between mother and son; Jesus' mother, like his family, thinks him crazy.[44] The earliest Gospel also knows no legendary story of Jesus' birth, says nothing about a virgin birth, of Mary standing by the cross, or Mary at the resurrection. It is only the later Gospels, depicting a believing, obedient Mary, which recount all that has become so deeply impressed on Christianity through the history of Christian art.[45] So already in the New Testament a distinction must be made between Mary as a historical figure and Mary as a symbolic figure[46] – as virgin, mother, bride, queen, intercessor.[47]

- According to the testimony of the New Testament Mary is above all the mother of Jesus. As a human being and a mother she is a witness to his true humanity. And this testimony to Jesus' humanity is not in contradiction with the faith also expressed in the New Testament, that Jesus' existence can ultimately be explained only in the light of God, has its deepest origin in God; that for believers he is the Son sent by God and chosen by God.[48]

- Mary is the example and model of Christian faith. Already according to the evangelist Luke, her faith, which is not spared the sword of offence, division and contradiction, and which experiences its greatest tribulation in the face of the cross, is in fact exemplary for Christian faith.[49] So Mary does not display any special faith, any special insight into the mysteries of God. Rather, her faith, too, undergoes a history and thus marks out the way of Christian faith.

- Mary points to the cause of her Son, to the cause of Jesus of Nazareth. Mary's cause is none other than Jesus' cause, which is God's cause. Here too Luke has set the right emphases. Mary's key words 'Fiat' and 'Magnificat' still make sense today. Mary praises a God who 'casts down the mighty from their thrones and exalts the lowly'.[50] And Mary's son, Jesus, does not have 'typically male' or 'patriarchal' features. Mary's son is more the friend of women, whom he calls to follow him as disciples and helpers, among them Mary Magdalene, who was venerated in the early communities as an intimate friend of Jesus.[51]

So those who attack the discrimination against women in the church which has lasted since the Middle Ages cannot appeal to Miriam/Mary and her son. No commands for women to be silent or submissive issue from the lips of Mary and Jesus. Neither knows any 'Eve myth' which makes women responsible for all the evil in the world. Neither knows any vilification of sexuality, any degradation of the woman as an object of pleasure or defamation as a universal seductress. Nor does either know any law of celibacy, though strikingly Jesus was unmarried; nor do they know any fixation on marriage. To this degree the apostle Paul interpreted the cause of Mary and Jesus sympathetically when he wrote about Christ, the exalted Lord, 'For freedom he has set us free.'[52] And 'Where the Spirit of this Lord blows, there is freedom.'[53] In the sphere of this freedom there is no place for sexual discrimination, devaluation of women, making sex taboo, emotionality, feminine corporeality, submission to a male hierarchy. In the sphere of this freedom which Christ embodies, 'there is neither male nor female, for you are all "one", in Christ Jesus.'[54]

But the crisis of papalism, Marianism and celibacy, which is manifest today even to traditional Catholics, was already developing in the late Middle Ages and at the beginning of the sixteenth century led to Martin Luther's Reformation.

# 4  Women at the Time of the Reformation

After the Gregorian Reform in the eleventh century and the breakthrough of the Roman Catholic paradigm in Western Christianity, no event in Western Christianity went deeper and proved more momentous than the Lutheran Reformation. In the sixteenth century Martin Luther initiated a new era: a further paradigm shift for the church, theology and Christianity generally, away from the Roman Catholic paradigm of the Middle Ages (P III) to the evangelical paradigm of the Reformation.

## Luther's fundamental impulse for reform

Martin Luther wanted a return to the gospel. At that time there were countless church traditions, laws and authorities: for Luther the criterion for what was Christian was 'scripture alone'. There were countless saints and official mediators to God: for Luther the mediator was 'Christ alone'. And countless works of piety and efforts to attain salvation were prescribed: for Luther men and women are justified 'by faith alone, by grace alone'.

Luther's critical new beginning had revolutionary consequences:

- He criticized the Latin sacrifice of the mass and private masses, therefore preaching was now central in worship. So too was a communal celebration of the eucharist purged of the notion of sacrifice (and using ordinary bread) in the vernacular. The laity too received communion from the chalice; in some places daily preaching replaced the daily mass.

- He criticized offices in the church, which had in fact suppressed the one Lord and Mediator Jesus. So he did away
  with the concept of priesthood as a hierarchy appointed
  by God, and of divine elements in church law. Instead he
  strengthened a sense of community and the awareness
  that offices in the church are ministries, the offering of
  service (the pastor stood at the eucharistic table in black
  robes, facing the congregation).
- He criticized monasticism and begging with a religious
  sanction. Instead he emphasized that worldly professions
  were divine callings and that even the lowliest work was
  of equal value: it had its dignity, indeed it was worship.
- He criticized those church traditions which were not
  justified by scripture, together with the pious works of
  everyday Catholic life, and therefore rejected the veneration of saints, the prescription of fasts, pilgrimages,
  processions, masses for the soul, the cult of relics, holy
  water and amulets. He abolished many festivals, above all
  Corpus Christi.
- Finally, Luther also criticized the law of celibacy as not
  being in keeping with the gospel, since it devalued sexuality, women, marriage and family and violated the freedom
  of Christians. He therefore also fundamentally affirmed
  marriage for priests and revalued marriage generally (not
  as a sacrament but as a 'secular-holy thing', solemnly
  performed in the church).[1]

## The changed situation of women

Did this Reformation also have consequences for the status and
role of women in the church and society? Did the equality of
man and woman in God's sight asserted in the apostle Paul's
letter to the Galatians (3.28) really exist? In other words, was the
true equality of women with men in the spirit of the New Testament, which was already hindered in the early church (P II), as

we saw, finally achieved under the auspices of the Reformation? Given all the differences of country, status, education, orientation of faith and personal circumstances of individual women, an answer to this question in the framework of our paradigm analysis will inevitably be very basic.

First of all it has to be recognized that the position of women, not only in the church but also in society, was changed positively by the paradigm shift which came about with the Reformation. For what characterized the new constellation (P IV) in which women now had to live in the territories of the Reformation? If we bear in mind the earlier account of women in the Roman Catholic mediaeval paradigm (P III) we can immediately understand how epoch-making the changes were:

- The mediaeval priority of celibacy was now replaced by the revaluation of marriage, the primacy of priestly ordination by that of everyday family life, the ideal of the nun by that of the housewife and mother, the vilification of sexuality by its affirmation as a natural human drive (to be satisfied in marriage, even if it did not serve to produce children).
- The monastic life was abolished along with the prohibition of marriage for priests: being married to a pastor opened up a completely new field of activity for a woman in a particular community (Luther's wife Catherine is an example).
- The cult of Mary, which idealized the virgin mother Mary at the expense of other dimensions of the feminine, retreated in favour of a secular ideal of women – which had already been taking shape since the lay culture (Minnesingers) of the twelfth century and the Renaissance.

In other words, for the whole area affected by the Reformation the world governed by priests, monks, nuns and their ideal of continence collapsed – and did so for good. A certain revaluation of communal monastic forms of life in more recent times is the exception that proves the rule. Nor can we overlook the change in social psychology represented by the structure of the community structure: now that pastors were married, the customary conscious or unconscious interest of the female part of the community in the one unmarried 'clergyman' (pastor or monk) disappeared, as did the often conscious or unconscious distancing of the male part of the community.

## Fellowship of men and women

It was one of the numerous merits of Martin Luther that in his theology he saw humanity in its physical nature and sexuality more clearly than his predecessors; for Luther the fellowship of husband and wife and the relationship of wife to husband and children are a basic fact of human existence. The Protestant theologian Gerta Scharffenorth describes Luther's position like this:

- 'Man and woman as God's creatures are together created in the image of God; bodiliness and sexuality are not at their disposal; they are God's gift and are to be respected as such.'[2]
- A 'shared responsibility of man and woman' follows from the task given by God at creation: 'for creation, for the coherence of all spheres and for conditions worth living in for the generation to come'.[3] They perform this task predominantly in the state of fatherhood and motherhood, which is prior to and superior to all other spiritual and worldly states.
- By baptism, women and men are destined 'to become friends of Christ'.[4] As Luther put it: 'Since all baptized women are spiritual sisters of all baptized men, as they have the same sacrament, spirit, faith, spiritual gifts and possessions, they will be much closer friends in the spirit than through outward kinship.'[5]

So there is no doubt that Martin Luther also made a practical contribution to the revaluation of women, above all through his plea for the education and schooling of girls as well as boys – though this had been put previously and much more clearly by Thomas More and Erasmus: as in the latter's 1524 memorandum on schools.[6] At the same time there is evidence that women also collaborated independently in the development, dissemination and defence of Protestant doctrine and the building up of Protestant communities (Margarete Blaurer in community work, Argula von Grünbach in publicity, Elisabeth Kreuziger in writing hymns, and so on).[7] As we saw,[8] individual women had already played a leading role in the high and late Middle Ages above all as rulers (especially as widows) and abbesses. To this degree the role of Elizabeth I of England and some other women regents and nobility was not new. And yet – unfortunately all this is only half the truth.

### The structure of society – still patriarchal

This indisputable progress must not mislead us: in the Reformation paradigm too, the social structure remained utterly patriarchal.[9] Of Luther's important thoughts about the brotherliness and sisterliness, the friendship, of men and women in Christ, all that was in fact left was the duty to marry. Despite all the new possibilities of activity for women, nothing changed in their role of being subordinate to men. The hierarchical structure of obedience (man-woman, parents-children, master-servants) was preserved. Marriages were still arranged by parents. The wife remained economically, legally and politically dependent on her husband, and the choice of her spouse was usually made for practical reasons. In any case, the constant surplus of women did not make things easier for them. And though since the late Middle Ages they had had a share in civic freedoms and greater possibilities of vocational fulfilment in crafts, trade and business (and also as women doctors), they by no means yet had the same rights or the same rewards.

Moreover it was not just in society that the gender-specific division of work and the stereotyping of the role of the sexes was maintained, to the disadvantage of women. Within the Reformation churches, too (Zinzendorf in pietism was the great exception), women by no means had the same share in 'sacrament, spiritual gifts and possessions'. Women still had no say in state, education and the church. On the contrary, under the sway of seventeenth-century Protestant orthodoxy, because of the wars, the economic recession and the increased competition for work outside the home, they were once again limited to the narrow household sphere. To what extent?

- Women continued to be excluded from all important church offices; they were accepted only as catechists and church servants.
- Not only the administration of the sacraments by women, but also preaching by women, which was practised in sects in the Middle Ages and called for by some humanist scholars, was normally forbidden.
- Space for unmarried women who had formally lived a safe, meaningful existence in convents had now disappeared, along with possibilities for educational activity, and thus unmarried women lost this basis for an independent life.
- At the same time, however, women's self-esteem was strengthened by religious instruction and the familiarity with scripture which had become possible.

## Women in Calvinism and Anglicanism

As the American historian Jane Dempsey Douglass of Princeton has emphasized in an instructive study,[10] in principle all this also applies to the sphere of Calvinism. Calvin, too, continued the patristic mediaeval tradition. For him, too, the spiritual equality of women with men (on the basis of the same spiritual soul, the same grace in this life and the same consummation through the resurrection) went with the social inequality of women and their subjection to men. To this degree, even with Calvin, Christianity by no means brought emancipation in the modern sense of the world.

And yet we should also see that unlike Augustine and Thomas Aquinas, Calvin (following the most famous physician of antiquity, Galen) rejected the Aristotelian view that the woman plays no active biological role in the formation of a foetus. Although even in the sixteenth century there was still widespread doubt about the physical robustness and intellectual power of women, slowly a consensus formed against Aristotle, that a woman was more than a 'defective man'.

At any rate, Calvin no longer argued in terms of physical nature when he spoke out against the ordination of women. Differing again from Thomas Aquinas, who denied women a natural capacity for the priesthood and in the light of biology and the divine law argued against women holding public office in the church, Calvin appealed 'only' to the human, church or state legal order. While this still had the same result as far as women were concerned (and to this degree Calvin is no champion of the ordination of women), it did have the decisive advantage that the possibility of changing this human ordinance could no longer be disputed with biological arguments, at least in principle. Moreover it was then adapted later to changed times.

How different the role of the woman could be, depending on her country, confession and historical situation, becomes evident as soon as one looks at more specific research. This is attested by individual studies of 'Women in Protestant History' (Anabaptists, Quakers and Methodists!).[11] The Australian historian Patricia Crawford has also demonstrated it for England between 1500 and 1720 in connection with women and religion.[12] Her investigation is illuminating not least because she discusses in context individual women already investigated in earlier research, who played an important role in connection with the English Reformation – like Henry VIII's second wife Anne Boleyn, who as guardian of bishops with a Protestant inclination, clergy welcoming reform and Protestant writers, along with other ladies was a key figure among the Reformers around the king and possibly advised him to dissolve the monasteries. And on the other side there was Margaret Roper, the married daughter of Thomas More, a highly educated woman who translated religious works from Greek and Latin[13] and thus also came to publish Erasmus' Latin Commentary on the 'Our Father'. And finally there was the controversial young Elizabeth Barton, a nun with prophetic gifts, who is to be seen against the background of the long tradition of women to whom visions were granted.[14] She headed the opposition to Henry VIII's second marriage, was executed without a trial in 1534, and thus was the first woman martyr for the traditional faith.

Nuns generally fared much worse than monks when their convents were dissolved; because monks were ordained, they could earn a living as diocesan clergy. Women like the Protestant Countesses of Suffolk and Richmond also played a major role in the time of Edward VI, not to mention the two queens who followed later, the Catholic Mary who called for the dismissal of all bishops' and priests' wives, and Elizabeth I, who restored the independence of the Church of England from Rome.

But here, too, the other side of the coin must be considered. The classical exponent of Anglican theology, Richard Hooker, still held the customary view that women had a weaker capacity for judgment by virtue of their sex. Indeed in Anglicanism the age-old theme of the special proneness of women to heresy still persisted. Women who attempted to challenge male power could at any time be accused of violating the divine order and endangering morals.

## Emancipation in the 'sects'?

Women played a special role in particular in the religious radicalism of the Presbyterian republican phase between 1640 and 1660, not of course because their capacity for judgment was weakened but on the contrary because with clear judgment they wanted a reformed church, and because more possibilities for activity would be granted them after the collapse of church control. A similar development had taken place a century earlier on the European continent in the Peasants' War and in the Baptist movement.[15] Now one could see and hear women teaching, preaching, celebrating the liturgy and engaging in mission. Many had joined the newer communities like the Quakers (the most significant of them was Margaret Fell, the 'mother of Quakerism'[16]). And their role differed from that of the sixteenth-century Protestant and Catholic martyrs: 'The conflicts of seventeenth-century women were conflicts with local authorities, pastors, justices of the peace and official judges. They adopted a public role but they were not martyrs, although many of them endured prison, physical punishment and violence for the sake of their faith.'[17]

But this, too, should not lead us to exaggerate the role of women in radical Protestantism. 'It would be anachronistic to suggest that women had found "emancipation" in the sects. It should not surprise us that the customary views of the nature and place of women in the world remained essentially the same during the revolutionary period of the 1640s and 1650s.'[18] Not only did the economic possibilities remain limited, but so did views about the role of women, sexuality and childbearing. 'So the sects did not offer a fundamentally different view of women from that of the Anglican Church or society generally.'[19] Only slowly did 'the churches develop towards accepting women as partners with equal rights', and there was a 'growing readiness to allow them to speak in the churches, which finally in the most recent decades has led to a gradual acceptance of the ordination of women'.[20]

However, on one point England came off better: here too up to the end of the seventeenth century there was a belief in witches; but compared with the European continent (and Scotland) far fewer people were persecuted in England. The question is not unimportant for our paradigm analysis. How is this terrible witch-craze to be explained?

## Women as witches

Even now it is not completely clear how this witch-craze is to be understood. It emerged in bursts at particular times and in particular places, interestingly enough, hardly at all in southern Italy and Spain; very little in England, Ireland, Scandinavia, on the north German plain, in Bavaria and also Eastern Europe; but very widely above all in France, Northern Italy, the Alpine countries, the rest of Germany, the Benelux states and Scotland.[21] How indeed are we to explain these mass phenomena, in which 80 to 90 per cent of those affected were women? Certainly Christianity had always had it in for witches; and the statement in the Hebrew Bible, 'You shall not allow a sorceress to live' (Ex. 22.18), had been the death of many witches. But 'witch' means substantially more than sorceress, and the trial of a witch substantially more than the trial of someone performing malicious magic (*maleficium*). In the high Middle Ages the notion of people who flew through the air by night was still being combated as a pagan error.

So the question is, how are we to explain the fact that by far the vast majority of Christians from the fifteenth century, and above all in the period of the Reformation and Counter-Reformation, no longer believed in the existence of individual sorceresses but – in a combination of different motives – did believe in a diabolical conspiracy, a new sect and highly dangerous heretical movement of witches, of malicious, lustful, devilish women who had powers over nature? According to the well-known pattern of interpretation on the part of those who believed in witches, a whole horde of women was said to have

- made a pact with the Devil, almost a covenant of marriage with the Devil, abjuring God;
- consorted with the Devil, having slept with the Devil (usually or often) to seal the pact;
- conjured up the Devil, an evil magic damaging the harvest and other aspects of life and killing animals or human beings;
- danced with the Devil, engaging in nocturnal orgies (witches' sabbath) with other witches.

The Tübingen exegete Herbert Haag, who has done a great service in combating the belief in the Devil still rampant today, remarks that 'the church with its doctrine of the Devil' provided the 'theological justification' for the elimination of supposed witches:

> Had the Devil not been developed into an overpowering figure, such an apparatus of extermination could not have been set up, and the wave of purges would not have found this echo in a people tormented by fear of the Devil. But as it was, the stake was the simplest and at the same time the most effective means of coping with the crisis.[22]

In church history (not to mention dogmatics), where it is not largely suppressed the witch-craze is often mentioned only in passing and not treated comprehensively. It was rightly brought into the centre of research by the women's movement of the 1970s. Witchcraft generally had fatal consequences for women: a destruction of the culture and the solidarity which women took for granted, a breakdown in the transmission of specifically feminine knowledge of women's own bodies and total submission to patriarchal domination. Once again, is there a conclusive explanation of all this?

## Who was to blame for the witch-craze?

It is not enough to explain the witch-craze with reference to the use of drugs (states of intoxication), the mass consumption of which cannot be proved; or to mental illness, which similarly does not explain the mass phenomenon; or even to a sup-pressed cult of Diana (fertility cult), which at best can be verified only in particular places or regions. On the other hand it is beyond dispute that there would have been no trials of witches without a popular superstition with a pagan stamp; without misogyny, the Inquisition and torture. However, there was superstition, misogyny, Inquisition and torture even before the witch trials, so the question must be asked: what else? Who was to blame for this development? A survey of research into witches shows that no monocausal explanation of the mass trials of witches is possible, and that the responsi-bility, as far as we can still see, lies with theologians and the mendicant orders, with the pope and the curia, the emperor and state power, and finally also with church people. To discuss these briefly:

1. In the face of the great heretical movements of the thir-teenth century, Scholastic theologians, especially Thomas Aquinas, developed an extensive demonology in which, fol-lowing Augustine, the doctrine of a pact with the Devil was used as a basis for a theory of superstition.[23] What had formerly been combated as pagan superstition was now incorporated into the theological system. And it was again two Dominican theologians, the Inquisitors for upper Germany and the Rhineland, Heinrich Institoris and (at least he put his name to it) Jacob Sprenger, who first of all overcame the inhibitions against belief in witches and witch trials that were widespread among the people and the clergy. They did this with their perni-cious handbook on witches, the *Malleus maleficarum* (*Hammer of the Witches*).[24] With a forged endorsement from the theologi-cal faculty of Cologne, between 1487 to 1669, in around 30

editions, it had a tremendous circulation and became the standard work for theologians, lawyers and physicians and for spiritual and secular courts. In the first part the concept of the witch was focussed on women with a series of quotations (some of them forged) from the Bible and classical authors; the second part specified all the abominations of witches; while the third part provided guidelines for punishment.

2. Papacy and curia. It was the popes who, as we saw, from the thirteenth century institutionalized and intensified the persecution of heretics and also assumed a connection between heresy and magic, both the work of the Devil. But it was then the Renaissance Pope Innocent VIII who as early as 1484, at the request of the two Dominicans mentioned above, promulgated his notorious bull against witches, *Summis desiderantes* (about which Denziger keeps quiet![25]), and thus gave the papal blessing to the novel doctrine of witches. Under threat of excommunication the 'beloved sons' were commanded not to hinder the interrogation of suspected witches by the Inquisition. And this unfortunate bull was then promptly made a preface to the 1487 *Hammer of the Witches*. So the pope and curia played a key part in the origination, legitimation and continuation of the mass trials of witches in Europe. The papal Inquisition, no less concerned with the persecution of heretics, provided the instrument which was now used against women: some denunciations, then instead of a public accusation by a private person, a secret investigation (Inquisition) by the authorities, torture to force a confession, and finally death by fire.

3. The emperor and the secular authorities. The legal basis for the mass implementation of witch trials was created by the Emperor Charles V's new (Roman) procedural law of 1532 (the 'Carolina'). Now the Inquisition process was carried out completely by the state. The guidelines for the trials of witches were so vague and varied that in practice almost anyone could be caught up in the inescapable millstones of the machinery of the

Inquisition. A mere rumour was often enough. But as this was an 'exceptional crime' (*crimen exceptum*), torture could also be used, without the restrictions provided for elsewhere by the lawyers. The consequence was that the names of alleged accomplices (known from the witches' dance) were extracted by indescribable torture, and a new spiral of trials was set in motion. Cruel ordeals for witches (by water and the needle) were also customary. Complete confession usually led to the death penalty, and recantation to renewed torture (sometimes tenfold), of unspeakable human cruelty. For a long time the death penalty was primarily carried out by burning; after 1600 usually by beheading. This terror lasted decade after decade, and was to reach its climax only after the first wars of religion between 1560 and 1630.

4. Church people themselves. As the majority of victims came from the lower classes in the country (the nobility were exceptions), it is generally assumed that some denunciations came from local communities. Simple village gossip, a person who looked abnormal or behaved abnormally, hatred, envy, enmity or avarice could be the beginning of 'petitions' to the authorities for protection from witches. The authorities would then set the whole machinery in motion. However, the background to this is the archaic anxiety about magical knowledge and practices which was so widespread among the people. This leads us to ask:

### Why the witch-craze?

Today, little can be said in detail with any precision about the ultimate psychological and political motives for the persecution of witches. Scholars mention a whole series of motives:

- the reactions of peasant workers to the bitterness and cursing of individual women;

- patriarchal anxieties about solitary women and their often quite real knowledge of medicine and contraception;
- the hostile attitude of the trained doctors (who first appeared with the universities), as opposed to popular medicine and the midwives and healers with no professional training who had been available to the people all down the centuries, with their often well-tried and traditional 'secret knowledge' (especially about giving birth, birth control and healings of all kinds);
- women as scapegoats for impotence and barrenness, for the failure of harvests, disease among cattle and catastrophe, sickness and death;
- a general xenophobia replacing hostility to the Jews (which after all the expulsions largely lacked any focus);
- the sexual obsessions and fantasies of celibate church Inquisitors who showed interest in the alleged perversions, obscenities and orgies (even with demons) of women with an insatiable lust, vilifying the witches as followers of Satan, so that they became a dark feminine principle (this was compensated for on the other side by the idealization of women in Mary – above the senses, pure and conceiving without a stain);
- the reaction of the church hierarchy and the absolutist authorities to an underground, uncontrollable popular culture;
- the confessionalizing which was interested in a far-reaching disciplining of the thought and behaviour of subjects.

For a long time the trials of witches were the subject of confessional apologetics and polemics: each side attempted to accuse the other of having the most black marks on its record. This was a vain enterprise, given the fact that belief in demons and witches was largely common to both Catholics and Protestants. Even if the *Hammer of the Witches* was increasingly attacked in detail, the regrettable fact has to be noted that not only within the mediaeval paradigm (P III) but also within the new Reformation paradigm (P IV), no one thought of examining belief in demons and witches critically, as one might have expected with the new orientations on the gospel. If the Catholic side was burdened by the long tradition of the persecution of heretics and witches, the Protestant side was burdened by the lack of any outrage against this inhuman and un-Christian craze.

If present-day scholarship, while no longer thinking in terms of millions of victims, at any rate reckons that there were at least 100,000 executions (and further punishments like banishment and open contempt); if, at any rate, it is clear 'that with the exception of the persecutions of the Jews these trials led to the greatest mass killing of human beings by other human beings in Europe which were not the result of war',[26] and if it is clear that despite all the denunciation of women by women this was a 'mass killing of women by men',[27] since men served as specialists, theologians and lawyers, as judges and executioners, we have to ask why at least from the Protestant side there was no vigorous protest against the witch-craze and the trials and burnings of witches – in the name of the freedom of Christians and the urgings of conscience.

It was above all the brave Jesuit and confessor to the witches, Friedrich von Spee, who in 1631 with his anonymously published work *Cautio criminalis* or *Legal Objections to the Witch Trials*[28] attacked all these goings-on, though with little success. At the beginning of the seventeenth century, in the course of the Enlightenment, the Protestant lawyer Christian Thomasius attacked the idea of pacts with the Devil and the whole sorry business of judgments on witches. Now he already found much support from the public. Whereas the mass trials in the United Netherlands had ended soon after 1600 and in France in 1650, in the German empire they ended only around 1680. It is commonly thought that the last burning of a witch was that of

Anna Schwägelin in 1775, in Catholic Kempten, but there were still mass burnings in Brandenburg in 1786. In other words, it was not the Reformation but the Enlightenment which put an end to the witch-craze, and the trials and burnings of witches.

# 5 Women in Modernity and Postmodernity

It is amazing how quickly in modernity Europeans were able to get a grasp of the world. They were able to take successively under their own control much, indeed almost everything, for which formerly God and superhuman, other-worldly powers had been held responsible. Rationality, freedom, coming of age were the slogans, first in Europe and then also in North America. Human beings were lords of themselves and lords of nature – this was a self-definition which was to lead to them having power over the world (with all the positive and negative consequences which could not yet be foreseen).

There is no doubt about it: this was a cultural revelation which even now is still seen in a negative light by parts of the Roman Catholic church. But viewed from the perspective of the secular world it represents incomparable progress.

- Incomparable progress in science: philosophy and the natural sciences change. They no longer operate with dogmatic assumptions but with facts of experience. Historiography no longer remains a subdivision of rhetoric or ethics, but becomes a separate discipline.
- A completely new ordering of society. Religious tolerance and freedom of belief are grounded in natural law. Ideas like constitutional law and the abolition of the privileges of clergy and the nobility arise. Science and art, industry and trade are officially encouraged and the schools are reformed.
- A revaluation of the individual. Innate human rights are to be codified and put under the protection of the state: the right to life, freedom and property along with a social and political emancipation of the citizen.

- A transition from an agricultural to an industrial society: an epoch-making revolution in the sphere not only of technology, of the processes of production, of the production of energy, of transport and the markets, but also in the social structures and mentality of the age. By the sharing of work, specialization, mechanization, rationalization and later automation of production, tremendous technological progress is achieved for the masses, though the consequence of this is a rise in social revolutions and crises.

If we look back at the revolutionary thrust of modern times which has just been analysed, we see that the situation of women is a most ambivalent one.

## The philosophical revolution and women

The philosophical revolution and the atmosphere of rationality which followed from it are doubtless responsible for the ending during the course of the seventeenth and eighteenth centuries of the witch-craze which was still virulent in the Reformation paradigm and which I reported at length. At the same time, from the seventeenth century, in the upper classes, starting in France, there were *femmes savantes*, highly educated women, who became the models for the aristocracy and the middle class: the salons of such ladies were meeting places for the cultural intelligentsia.

But that still says little about the real equality of men and women in theory and practice. And how firmly cemented the traditional understanding of roles was is shown by the fact that even the intellectual philosophical or literary élite hardly made any difference here (some philosophers like Descartes, Spinoza, Leibniz and Kant were in fact bachelors). For Kant, woman above all embodies 'the beautiful', while man embodies 'the exalted': 'laborious learning or painful brooding' would 'weaken the charm by which they (women) exert their great power on the other sex'.[1] Even for Rousseau, whose novel about education, *Émile*, was to influence educational theories so much in the subsequent period, the relationship between man and woman is one of control: the woman needs only as much education as is pleasing to the man. And in his famous 'Song of the Bell', which had such a tremendous influence on the middle classes of the nineteenth and twentieth centuries, Friedrich Schiller – here hardly differing from Goethe – assigned the woman once and for all a role in the silent inner room of the 'home', sending the man out alone 'into hostile life'. At any rate women could get themselves something of a modern education from the magazines and newspapers which were appearing at this time, and at the theatre.

It was the early Romantic movement which set contrary accents here, redefined the role of the sexes, fully affirmed the unity of spirituality and the senses in love, and recognized the happy relationship between man and woman in free self-fulfilment as a presupposition for a full life. Mention should be made here of Friedrich Schlegel, and also of Friedrich Schleiermacher, who did more than any other theologian to advance the theology of the sexes and emphasized the significance of the collaboration of male and female forces in the Christian community. But the weakness of all the Romantic new beginnings, which in any case hardly came out in public life in the atmosphere of the Restoration, was evident: the economic and legal conditions under which the mass of women lived in the rising industrial society remained unilluminated. Even the long book by Johann Jakob Bachofen, *Matriarchal Law* (1861),[2] which took up Schlegel in a belief that it was possible to demonstrate historically a matriarchal form of society before the state, later replaced by a period of patriarchy, was in no way intended as support for the legal and political emancipation of women. Whatever may be thought of the hypothesis of an early matriarchy put forward in this book, which for various reasons made many enemies, only later did historians and philosophers of culture become aware how much women had been kept back behind men in past millennia (even in the Bible), indeed how often they had been instrumentalized and dominated.

## The political revolution and women

Both in America and in France the political revolution brought a declaration of the Rights of Man which 'really' should also have embraced women. But since in English and French '*homme*/man' can mean both 'human being' and 'male', these rights of man were very soon interpreted merely as the rights of males, especially where they were the right to vote, the right to property, coalition or speak in public. The women involved in the French Revolution who were members of the newly formed revolutionary women's associations under the leadership of Olympe de Gouges and Rosa Lacombe composed their own 'Declaration of the Rights of Women and Citizenesses' as early as 1791. In it, Article 10, for example, calls for the right of freedom to speak publicly, giving as the reason: 'Woman has the right to ascend the scaffold. She must equally have the right to ascend the (speaker's) tribune' (in England, Mary Wollstonecraft called for civil rights for women for the first time in 1792).[3] But the National Convention in Paris, utterly dominated by males, condemned such efforts. It wanted to be rid of the king of the country, but by no means to dethrone the king at home. So the legal dependence of the woman on the man, father or husband, was maintained, and women were only indirectly granted civil rights.

Thus on the whole women had to wait until the end of the First World War to be given the vote in the leading industrial countries – the main demand of the early women's movement: in New Zealand (as early as 1893), Finland, Norway and Denmark this happened before the War, then in the Netherlands and the Soviet Union in 1917, in Great Britain in 1918, in

Germany in 1919, and in the United States in 1920 (France would only follow in 1944 and Switzerland in 1971!). However, we should note that even the constitutional establishment of equal rights by no means automatically brought equality in the sphere of the family or the workplace, and often it did not even result in the active collaboration of large numbers of women in parties, parliaments and governments, not to mention law courts, educational establishments and industry.

## The industrial revolution and women

However, as early as the nineteenth century the industrial revolution had changed the status of women more deeply than any former historical developments, though initially more in a negative way. It was the new technological conditions of the production processes which necessitated the participation of women in the work. Spinning, knitting, weaving, stitching and other tasks moved outside the house in a quite unplanned way, into the factories and the cities. Consequently many women lost household tasks, sources of income and conversation, and with the growing need for labour were forced to become the cheaper and in some respects the more skilled rivals of men in factories. But this brought them into a new dependent relationship and often caused great distress, while the family as a group which had lived and worked together fell apart.

At the same time, though, efforts to give women an equal place alongside men began. However, it was not the churches which took the lead here, but Liberals and especially Socialists, who engaged in fundamental reflection on the situation of women in the conditions of production in an industrial society, analysed this closely and combined it with a passionate criticism of bourgeois society.

Thus it is not chance that a section on the situation of women was already included in the Communist Manifesto of 1848. In their document Marx and Engels gave a sharp answer to the charge from bourgeois society that the Communists wanted to introduce a 'community of women': 'The bourgeois sees in his wife a mere instrument of production. He hears that the instruments of production are to be exploited in common, and, naturally, can come to no other conclusion than that the lot of being common to all will likewise fall to the women. He has not even a suspicion that the real point aimed at is to do away with the status of women as mere instruments of production. For the rest, nothing is more ridiculous than the virtuous indignation of our bourgeois at the community of women which they pretend is to be openly and officially established by the Communists. The Communists have no need to introduce community of women. It has existed almost from time immemorial. Our bourgeois, not content with having the wives and daughters of the proletarians at their disposal, not to speak of common prostitutes, take the greatest pleasure in seducing each other's wives. Bourgeois marriage is in reality a system of wives in common and thus, at the most, what the Communists might possibly be reproached with, is that they desire to introduce in substitution for a hypocritically concealed, an openly legalized community of women. For the rest, it is self-evident that the abolition of the present system of production must bring with it the abolition of the community of women springing from that system, i.e. of prostitution both public and private.'[4]

So Marx and Engels, taking up the ideas of L. H. Morgan and Bachofen, and explicitly defending the possibility of divorce without divorce proceedings, were concerned radically to change the status of women as 'mere instruments of production' and under the conditions of an industrial society in which work was shared to grant them equal rights and equal dignity with men.[5] Here the central idea of the Socialist interpretation of the emancipation of women was that the revolutionary liberation of the proletariat would almost automatically bring with it the liberation of women. Subsequently, one could also read this in August Bebel's (1840–1913) book on *The Woman and Socialism*

(1883),[6] which with its dozens of editions was to shape the attitudes of Socialists and Communists to the women's question in the future. But even in the context of Socialism, including social democracy, it took a long time for people to lose their illusions that the social and the sexual revolutions were contemporaneous. After all, even the Socialists (down to the student movement of 1968) were quick to castigate social exploitation without considering the exploitation in their own families.

Of course the emancipation of women was also advanced from the non-socialist side. Thus as early as 1848 there was a women's congress in the USA which called for the recognition of women as citizens with equal rights. The movement for political emancipation in Great Britain began after 1860. It was the philosopher John Stuart Mill who put the first proposal for giving an active vote to women in Parliament in 1867. In Germany, the Universal German Women's Association was founded in 1865, and was predominantly concerned with questions of women's work and the education of women; now the daughters of the middle class were often under pressure to earn their living and thronged into the places of higher education. But here we are programmatically interested more in the question of Christianity: how did theology and the church react to the new situation for women in the nineteenth century?

### Have the churches hindered or encouraged the emancipation of women?

Despite all efforts at inner renewal and social action, the main focus was on reintegrating those who had been alienated from the church into the old social order, viewed as a body in which there were different classes (with a renewal of the professional classes and the demand for a class parliament as opposed to the modern party state),[7] by means of a programme of re-Christianization carried on by the church. Thus the church was to hold together all social classes and states in harmony and give them a spiritual stamp by a disposition towards love and mutual service. And although there were failures in this idealistic enterprise of re-Christianizing among both the middle classes and the proletariat, and hardly any progress was made in the face of religious indifference, the rejection of the church, agnosticism and atheism, there was a failure to see that such a policy of reintegration into a former paradigm (whether P III or P IV) was self-deception. (And the pope at the beginning of the twenty-first century who again dreams of a 're-evangelization' or 're-Christianization' of Europe has yet to understand this.)

To this degree I can only agree with Martin Greschat's final conclusion:

> So this theoretical and practical alternative to modernity, developed comprehensively by Catholicism and supported pragmatically by Protestantism, which also shared the responsibility for it, essentially insisted that the church must remain itself, that it must concentrate on its essence grounded in revelation, and from this origin pervade and guide society with its spirit.

And this meant:

> At most the churches accepted the reality of social change, and thus the modern world, only partially, never in principle. They saw the whole world being affected by it, but not themselves. This distance from reality gave the churches everywhere on the one hand the courage and good conscience with which they could largely see themselves as standing above the parties, above all conflicts. But the selfsame fact was also to a considerable degree the reason for the growing ineffectiveness of this theology and this courage within modern European industrial society.[8]

Nowhere, perhaps, is it clearer that the traditional view advocated by the official church and theology that society must be governed by the church in decisive matters was no longer viable than in what has been wrongly abbreviated as the 'women's question'.

At least three general points may be made:

- The manifold women's movements which emerged in different countries at different times initially found hardly any support in the churches.
- In particular the Communist Manifesto of 1848 had hardly any effect on the churches in the first decades: its active working woman did not correspond to the traditional Christian model.
- The churches' efforts at the emancipation of women, which began very much later, hardly reached the level of women working in industry, but remained limited to the middle class.

However, whereas in the framework of former paradigms it was still easier to talk about the status and role of 'women' in general, this becomes almost impossible within the framework of the modern paradigm, since national conditions take so many forms.

## The situation in modern Catholicism

The situation is still most uniform in the Catholic-Romanic countries, where the Roman church government very effectively extended its opposition to modernity to the efforts of women to achieve emancipation. Even Pope Leo XIII, who was more open than his predecessors, felt compelled as late as 1885 in the encyclical *Immortale Dei* to declare that 'the man is set over the woman', with a literal quotation from Augustine (cf. P III): women are to be subject to their husbands 'in chaste and faithful obedience, not for the satisfaction of lust but for the procreation of the human race and for life together in the family'.[9]

It is true that in his famous encyclical on social ethics which appeared in 1891, *Rerum novarum*, the same pope then not only condemned in general terms the unlimited exploitation of workers by employers who treated human beings as things, but also specifically condemned heavy manual labour for children and women. But the reason he gave for this was that the female sex was 'by nature fitted for homework, and it is that which is best adopted at once to preserve her modesty and to promote the good bringing-up of children and the well-being of the family'.[10]

Thus, tied to the natural law doctrine of antiquity and the Middle Ages (cf. P III), the popes of the following period down to Pius XII still saw woman exclusively in terms of her 'natural disposition' as a mother, which now bound her to family and home. They could not perceive the thoroughgoing disadvantage, often oppression, suffered by women as a result of the pre-eminence of men which was the real challenge of modernity. As the Catholic social ethicist Stephan Pfürtner points out, 'A philosophy of essence and natural law derived the "essence of woman" from role relationships developed over history and from biological facts, and in turn made this the normative determination for female behaviour'; he sees the reason for this defective theory, which is highly pernicious in practice, in 'inadequate communication between theology and church government and the critical movements in the church and society of the time'. 'The pioneering ideas about emancipation from the bourgeois and socialist women's movement were hardly taken seriously in Catholicism, or largely repudiated.'[11]

In fact it was John XXIII who was the first to bring about a change with the encyclical *Pacem in terris* and the Second Vatican Council, which also had a liberating effect on the Catholic women's associations, though the question of contraception (first left undecided and then decided in the negative) proved a permanent burden and a reason for millions of women to leave the church.[12]

For the emancipation of women in the church the pontificate of John Paul II (since 1978) has meant a time of stagnation, if not regression. He has adopted rigorist positions on matters of birth control, abortion and homosexuality and proclaimed that it is the will of God and 'an infallible teaching of the church' that it is impossible for women to be ordained. In particular the refusal of the Catholic church in Germany to take part in the counselling which is legally required where there is a conflict of interests for pregnant women is still a heavy burden on relations with Rome and has severely damaged the moral credibility of the Polish pope there. Once again, it is the women who suffer.

## The situation in modern Protestantism

The situation of women in modern Protestant countries is very much more complex, but increasingly, historical work is being done on it in most recent scholarship – in the face of all the silence over the role of women in Protestant church history, too. Moreover a collection of articles on the topic 'Women in Protestant History' which was published in the United States in 1985 appeared under the title *Triumph over Silence*.[13] The situation is the same in Germany, to which I must limit myself here for reasons of space; in many respects it may serve as an example for other Protestant countries.[14]

Moves by individual emancipated women at the beginning of the nineteenth century, Rachel von Varnhagen-Levin, Karoline von Günderrode or Bettina von Arnim-Brentano, were at first hardly noticed; indeed within the church they met more with reserve and criticism. So it was no wonder that representatives of the early women's movement in Germany before 1848 (Fanny Lewand, Malwida von Meysenburg, Luise Otto) and the later women's movement (above all Helene Lange, the president of the newly founded 'Alliance of German Women's Associations', 1894) turned their backs on the church: 'Disappointed by

Christianity, most of them never found their way back into a Christian congregation.'[15]

And yet the women's movement did not pass by the Protestant churches without any trace. Women involved in the church first became more active with the formation and development of the Protestant Diakonia movement (Hinrich Wichern, Theodor Fliedner and Wilhelm Löhe were the leading figures in this connection). This not only gave women a church office on the model of the early Christian community (as deaconesses): it also offered girls from socially weakened families and families impoverished by the process of industrialization tasks in which they could develop their capabilities and take responsibility even if they were unmarried. Men and women could work together in such voluntary associations without the usual scheme of male superiority and female subordination. It was not least Schleiermacher and his understanding of religion which stood in the background where there was an understanding in the church that assigned an important place to the collaboration of men and women.

But even in the deaconess communities, Protestant male 'hierarchs' legally retained male pre-eminence in important decisions and in representation in the outside world. Here we can detect influences from the Catholic women's congregations, which were dominated by male priests. In these circumstances, any interest on the part of the deaconesses (and the many pastors' wives) in equal rights for women in society was ruled out a priori. At first simply limited to charitable tasks (like the 'Association for the Care of the Poor and the Sick', founded by Amalie Sievekink in Hamburg in 1832), after the 1848 revolution this women's movement within Protestantism also dedicated itself to getting schooling and vocational training for girls and women in order to prepare them for functions in society and the state. It was the economist Dr Elisabeth Gnauck-Kühne, a sympathizer with Christian socialism, who then at a Protestant social congress in

1895 called for justice instead of mercy for women and made many men change their minds.

However, until very recently there has been far too little research into the more recent history of women who as Christians sought social responsibility in Germany, especially from the perspective of the women themselves. So in the Institute for Ecumenical Research of the University of Tübingen – as I already reported in connection with the patristic period (P II) – within the framework of the research project 'Women and Christianity' we investigated not only the situation of women in the first four Christian centuries but also the situation of Christian women in the nineteenth and twentieth centuries. A study by the historian Doris Kaufmann entitled *Women between Starting Point and Reaction. The Protestant Women's Movement in the First Half of the Twentieth Century* was the result of this research.[16] This study produced important results, particularly for our question, and I want to refer to them here. For especially in the history of Protestant women, a disregard of the dominant thought-patterns, like the division of society into a public and a private sphere, the former thought of as the man's sphere of activity and the second as the woman's, has proved successful. One of the important results of the research in this project was that, particularly within the framework of the church, the boundaries between these areas, which were often thought of as separate, were crossed, and women regularly invaded the 'public male sphere of the church'. This is particularly true of the German Protestant Women's Alliance, founded in 1899, which as a social movement involved in its contemporary environment was the main object of Doris Kaufmann's research.

It was possible to demonstrate that with reference to women's own exegesis of the biblical anthropology of the sexes and the definition of their tasks in this organization, women fought for new spheres of activity and responsibilities in church institutions and major Protestant organizations (e.g. the Inner

Mission and later also world mission) – and did so against not inconsiderable resistance within Protestantism and the church. They indefatigably called for the right to vote in church and commune and for payment for community social work. And these Protestant women also attempted to change the relationship between the sexes (and the power that went with it) throughout society, by attacking the prevalent moral norms in the question of prostitution with reference to the demands of the gospel.

Moreover, this Protestant group (in party-political terms quite a conservative one), which aimed at a comprehensive redefinition of the place of women in the state, achieved considerable successes for all Protestant women against the background of the general inter-confessional women's movement, and was able to make an essential contribution towards their 'emancipation'. Granted, it was only after the revolution of 1918 (which they repudiated) that the Protestant women achieved the right to vote in church and commune which they had asked for. But even before 1918 they were able to establish their own places of education (Social Women's Schools), run their own social work projects (homes for women in danger, unmarried mothers), appear in politics and get the Protestant public used to women speakers and women members of Congress. This organization for the first time gave Protestant women loyal to the church the possibility of dedicating themselves to women's rights over and above their honorary work in the community and in welfare work, which was all that was customary up to the turn of the century, without having to leave the religious sphere. On the contrary, the German Protestant Women's Alliance attempted to make the Christian message itself the starting point of its commitment to women. In the 1920s these efforts were to bear fruit but also to bring disappointments; however, here I shall not be going beyond the end of the First World War.

Something else that Doris Kaufmann's investigation demonstrates for the history of the Protestant women's movement, even in the first half of the twentieth century, must also be mentioned: while individual processes of emancipation which began by claiming to take seriously the 'liberating force of the gospel for women' succeeded, such experiences of strength and the capacity to win through remained limited to Protestant women at middle-class-bourgeois and aristocratic levels. Thus in its political and social action even the Protestant Women's Alliance ultimately could not cast off the interests of these classes – for all its proclamation of a women's solidarity with a Christian foundation going beyond the parties. The Protestant Women's Movement would not and could not achieve a general Christian social and political influence which transcended frontiers.

## The feminist movement

Developments in modernity between the seventeenth century and the First World War left Christianity with more problems than can be described here. But there are four problem fields where first the paradigm shift from modernity (P V) to postmodernity (P VI) becomes particularly clear and, secondly, Christianity in the new era is faced with enormous tasks.

These relate to various dimensions of reality:

- the cosmic dimension: human beings and nature (the ecological movement);
- the anthropological dimension: men and women (the women's movement);
- the socio-political dimension: rich and poor (fair distribution);
- the religious dimension: human beings and God (the ecumenical and interfaith movements).

It was necessary to wait until after the Second World War, indeed until the 1960s and 1970s, for the possibility of a new discussion throughout society and the church on equal rights and partnership between men and women which took into account the difference between the sexes. Here the catalysts were the World Council of Churches (founded 1948), the Second Vatican Council (1962–65) and the 1968 movement in America and Europe.

We can no longer fail to see that a new generation of women has grown up which more firmly than former generations insists that being a Christian and social emancipation are no longer contradictory. The gospel contains enough pointers for women not only to be assured of their own dignity in general, but also on their own rights to participate in all spheres of church and society, rights which in no way fall short of those of men.

This new generation of Christian women has created a new term for its self-confidence: 'feminist theology'.[17] This means that women no longer take over theological schemes developed by men without questioning them; their faith no longer reflects the borrowed experiences of men, but is a discovery of the reality of their own experience so that they begin to become subjects of their own theology. Only now is a theology being practised which takes up what Elisabeth Moltmann-Wendel once described like this: 'The emphasis should be not only on the freedom from which one comes (justification) but also on the freedom to which one goes. That means openness to new roles and lifestyle, to social change and all kinds of co-operation. The human right that comes from justification also still has an unfulfilled future for many people.'[18]

However, the church and theology had missed so many opportunities, and modern tendencies were so little supported by the church authorities, that so far only a minority of women had been reached by the reinterpretation of the role of the woman in church and society, although for a long time women had provided far more support locally for the church as an institution than men. Today it is becoming evident, not least in the question of women, to what extent meanwhile secularization has taken hold in the modern world. This is a secularization which began centuries ago, but which has become a mass phenomenon in most recent times.

So is not the current equal status of women an urgent necessity for postmodernity instead of the privileges which discriminate in favour of men? And what can the various religions, above all prophetic religion, contribute to a change of global consciousness in the postmodern paradigm on the basis of the religion of women? Can the religions contribute towards the implementation of political and social human rights and thus to the dimension of partnership between men and women?

## Questions to the churches

What may have been 'comprehensible' to the Hellenistic paradigm of the early church becomes completely incomprehensible when blatant or latent discrimination against women in the Christian churches is still justified and maintained today with an appeal to 'church tradition'. So here too – given the transition of our world from the modern to the postmodern paradigm – questions are raised for the future.[19] These questions must be put above all to the Orthodox and the Roman Catholic churches.

- By what right do the Orthodox and the Roman Catholic churches still refuse women an equal share in their activities, to the point of excluding them from the ministry of the church? Shouldn't traditional theological structures of legitimation, for example the argument that a woman cannot be a 'symbol of Christ', be questioned in the light of the original ethic of Jesus and the early Christian community?[20] Given the leading functions of women in the earliest church (as evidenced, say, by Phoebe and Prisca) and in view of the completely different position of women today in business, scholarship, culture, state and society, may the admission of women to the priesthood be postponed any longer? Weren't Jesus and the early church ahead of their time in the evaluation of women, so that churches which continue to prohibit the ordination of women lag far behind the gospel and the practice of other churches?

- The Methodist church was the first church to elect a woman to the office of bishop in 1980. It was followed by the Episcopal Church of the USA in 1989 and the Evangelical Lutheran Church in Germany in 1992. By what right do representatives of the Catholic and Orthodox churches threaten serious problems and difficulties for ecumenical 'dialogues'? Is it right for the ecumenical 'dialogue' between the churches to continue at the expense of the equal status of women? Rather, should not churches which reject the ordination of women to the office of bishop and priest self-critically examine their own practice in the light of the gospel and early church tradition? Is it not their rejection of the ordination of women that represents the real obstacle to the ecumenical movement?

- Isn't it time for the Orthodox and Catholic churches to concede that the Protestant, Anglican and Old Catholic churches are closer to the gospel on the question of the ordination of women than they are? Isn't the appeal to conservative 'sister churches' an excuse to hold up reform in their own churches? Isn't it time, in the spirit of the gospel, to end the practice of discrediting, defaming and discriminating against women and to offer them too the dignity that is their due in the church and to guarantee them an appropriate legal and social status?

## A fellowship of brothers and sisters, free and equal

The church of the future should no longer appear as a strong-hold of reaction against democracy. Rather, in the spirit of its founder it should be a fellowship in 'freedom, equality and brotherhood', the kind of community which I sketched in connection with the way in which the earliest church was ordered as a community (P I).

- The church should be a fellowship of the free! Is it legitimate for it to appear, rather, as an institution which exercises domination or even as a Grand Inquisitor? Doesn't this freedom need to be expressed in the shaping of the church as a fellowship, in such a way that its institutions and constitutions never again have an oppressive or repressive character or exercise the domination of one set of human beings by another? So the Christian church needs to be seen as a sphere of freedom made possible in the light of the gospel and at the same time as an advocate of freedom in the world.
- The church should be a fellowship of those who are in principle equal! Is it legitimate instead for it to appear as a church of classes, races and castes, or even as a church of clergy? Doesn't this equality need to be expressed in the shaping of the church fellowship, in such a way that the diversity of gifts and ministries are not levelled down by some mechanical egalitarianism, but rather that the very different members and groups are guaranteed equal fundamental rights, and the structures of the organization in no way encourage injustice and exploitation?
- The church needs to be a fellowship of brothers and sisters. Is it legitimate instead for it to be a system of domination under a patriarchal rule, in which people are prevented from coming of age by paternalism and a personality cult and (when it comes to holding office and

representation) the female sex is legally or *de facto*
excluded or marginalized? Doesn't the spirit of brotherhood and sisterhood need to be expressed in the
ordinances and social conditions of the church fellowship, in such a way that the democratic demands for the
greatest possible freedom and the best possible equality,
which fundamentally conflict, are reconciled in the solidarity of a community of brothers and sisters? The
Christian church needs to be seen as a sphere which
promotes brotherhood and sisterhood, not only for itself,
but for the whole world.

What concrete changes does such a major programme require?
Here, briefly, are some suggestions for a plan of action.

## Specific demands

I shall make some practical proposals for reform which need to
be put into practice as quickly and as thoroughly as possible by
the Christian churches. In fact I first proposed them around 25
years ago, but the need for action is still as great as ever.

It is not in the nature of Christian marriage for the wife to be
subject to her husband; the statements in the New Testament
about the submission of the wife (which mostly occur in the
later New Testament writings) need to be understood in the
light of the social and cultural situation of the time and translated critically in terms of our social and cultural situation
today. Many couples have discovered that a marriage in partnership is more in keeping with the dignity of human beings,
who as man and woman are created in the image of God.

Nor can a particular division of work be derived from the
nature of Christian marriage – say, that the wife should bring up
the children and the husband should go out to work. Bringing
up children, housework and having a job can be shared by both
husband and wife.

So the daughters of a family should be educated and trained for a profession in precisely the same way as sons. And sons should be just as prepared to help their parents and perform household tasks as daughters. A woman's professional life is certainly not the same thing as her emancipation. But in education and also in preaching, religious education and marriage counselling the possibilities for women should not almost exclusively (sometimes even with a reference to God's plan) be seen as an alternative between being a married housewife and being an unmarried religious. The wealth of opportunities and models for women in work should not be ignored.

Birth control, if practised in a responsible way, can contribute to a genuine emancipation of women, provided that it does not lead to the sexual exploitation of women and that the sexual revolution is not identified with the emancipation of women. Having fewer children can make it possible, particularly for women in the lower strata of society, to complete professional training, to co-ordinate a job with family life, and to be free of financial burdens and burdens at work.

In the controversial question of abortion it is necessary to take account not only of the rights of the foetus, but also of the physical and psychological health and social situation of the mother, and her responsibility to her family and especially to the children whom she is already looking after.

If the Catholic church, whose power structures and offices are entirely dominated by males, is to become a church for all people, women must be represented in all decision-making bodies: at parish, diocesan, national and global levels. A blatant example of the non-representation of women is the Roman Congregation for Religious Orders, which does not have a single woman member; according to present legislation even an ecumenical council can consist only of males and the pope can only be elected by males. None of this is a matter of divine law; it is purely human law.

The language of the liturgy should express the fact that the community consists of both women and men who in principle have equal rights. The 'brothers' and 'sons of God' should never be addressed exclusively and by themselves; the 'sisters' and 'daughters of God' should also be included, both brothers and sisters being 'children of God'.

The study of Catholic theology by women, who in many places gain only limited admission or are completely excluded, needs to be encouraged. Women should be admitted to full theological study so that the church and theology (not least ethics, and here again particularly sexual ethics) everywhere gain from the insights of women. Women theological students should be encouraged by the church institutions just as much as male theological students (through church scholarships, grants for academic work, etc.).

The women's religious orders have often been most effective in implementing the Second Vatican Council's principles of renewal, but often they have been hindered rather than helped by the official male church. Despite the lack of priests, women religious have been prevented from becoming the leaders of communities and so far they have been denied the financial means for an adequate education, while large sums of church money are spent on male candidates for the priesthood. Here help is urgently needed, not least in view of the rapid decline in membership of the religious orders.

In practice, celibacy for priests often leads to an unnaturally tense relationship between priests and women; women are often regarded merely as sexual beings and a sexual temptation to priests. Thus the prohibition of marriage for ordained men and the prohibition of ordination for women belong together: the ordination of women and complete collegial collaboration in those bodies in the church which exercise leadership and make decisions will not take place until clerical celibacy has been replaced with freely chosen celibacy by those who are truly called (to celibacy as well).

The reintroduction of the diaconate for women, which is

attested in the early church, which was first abolished in the Western church and which then disappeared in the Eastern church, is highly desirable. But this measure is not enough. Unless the admission of a woman to the diaconate also at the same time makes her admission to the presbyterate possible, this would not lead to equal rights for women, but rather to a postponement of their ordination. To allow the practice already existing in many Catholic communities, which is to be endorsed without qualification, of admitting women to liturgical functions (serving at mass, reading, distributing communion and preaching), can also be an important step on the way towards fully integrating women into church leadership. But even this does not make the demand for the full ordination of women superfluous.

There are no serious theological objections to women priests. The fact that the group of twelve was exclusively male must be understood in terms of the social and cultural situation of the time. The reasons that can be found in tradition for the exclusion of women (sin came into the world through a woman; woman was created second; women are not created in the image of God; women are not full members of the church; the taboo over menstruation) cannot appeal to Jesus. Rather, they bear witness to a fundamental theological defamation of women. In view of the way in which women functioned as leaders in the earliest church (Phoebe and Prisca) and in view of the completely different position of women today in business, scholarship and science, culture, state and society, the admission of women to the priesthood should not be further delayed. Jesus and the early church were ahead of their time in their valuation of women; today the Catholic church lags far behind its time and other Christian churches.

It would be a wrong understanding of ecumenism to delay reforms in the Catholic church like the ordination of women, which are long overdue, with reference to the greater restraint of conservative 'sister churches'. Instead of being used as an excuse, such churches should be invited to reform themselves; here some Protestant churches could serve as an example to the Catholic church. For a long time women in the Catholic church have been discredited and defamed in both theory and practice, while at the same time being exploited. It is time to give them their due dignity and an appropriate legal and social status in the church as well as in society.

## Conclusion

As I remarked earlier, it is now around 25 years since I made these proposals in a German journal.[21] Can we rejoice over success? Can we despair at failure? Here we have to differentiate in passing judgment. Much has changed, as far as individuals, married couples, communities and theological faculties have been able to change it. Changes have taken place in the partnership of men and women, the division of work, education and professional training for daughters and the preparation of sons for being fathers and sharing in household tasks, birth control, the language of worship, the presence of women representatives in many decision-making bodies at the parish and diocesan level, and the possibility for Catholic women to study theology.

But much for which the hierarchy has been responsible has not changed: legitimation for contraception, a differentiated view of abortion, the women representative in decision-making bodies at a national and global level, a renewal of women's religious orders, abolition of celibacy for the clergy, the reintroduction of the diaconate for women, the introduction of priesthood for women, and serious progress in ecumenism. So there is no reason to wonder at the constant resigned departure of women from the Roman Catholic church in particular, which can be demonstrated both statistically and empirically, and to shed crocodile tears over it.

I must soberly point out that if I had to wait another 25 years for the clergy to gain insight, I would presumably not live to see it, nor would others with me. *Speramus contra spem* – we hope against hope.

# Notes

## Abbreviations

LW  Luther's Works (standard English translation), 54 vols + intro., St Louis and Philadelphia, 1955–76.

*TRE Theologische Realenzyklopädie*, ed. G. Krause and G. Müller, 17 vols, Berlin 1977–.

WA  Weimarer Ausgabe (standard German edition of Luther's works), Weimar 1883–.

## 1. Women in Earliest Christianity

1.   For the sociology of the earliest community cf. M. Weber, *Ancient Judaism*, Glencoe, III, 1952, especially the appendix, 'The Pharisees', and above all G. Theissen, *Studien zur Soziologie des Urchristentums*, Tübingen ³1989, especially Part II, 'Evangelien'. However, the picture of Jesus the 'itinerant preacher' may not have been developed by just one strand of tradition (essentially the logia source Q). For the further social and political context cf. E. Stambaugh and D. L. Balch, *The New Testament and Its Social Environment*, Philadelphia 1986. For the origin of the church cf. H. Küng, *The Church*, London and New York 1968, B, 'The Coming Reign of God' (and the bibliography). Further theological works on the earliest community are: P. V. Dias, *Vielfalt der Kirche in der Vielfalt der Jünger, Zeugen und Diener*, Freiburg 1968; id., *Kirche. In der Schrift und im 2.Jahrhundert*, Freiburg 1974; G. Hasenhüttl, *Charisma. Ordnungsprinzip der Kirche*, Freiburg 1969; J. J. Becker et al., *Die Anfänge des Christen-*

*tums. Alte Welt und neue Hoffnung*, Stuttgart 1987 (especially the contributions by J. J. Becker, C. Colpe and K. Löning; M. Hengel, *The 'Hellenization' of Judaea in the First Century after Christ*, London and Philadelphia 1989; L. Schenke, *Die Urgemeinde. Geschichtliche und theologische Entwicklungen*, Stuttgart 1990; J. Roloff, *Die Kirche im Neuen Testament*, Göttingen 1993.

2.  *Contra Apionem* 2, 201; cf. J. Jeremias, *New Testament Theology*, Vol. I, London and New York 1971, 226.

3.  Cf. E. and F. Stagg, *Women in the World of Jesus*, Philadelphia 1978; E. Moltmann-Wendel, *The Women around Jesus*, London and New York 1982; F. Quéré, *Les femmes de l'évangile*, Paris 1982; J. Blank, 'Frauen in den Jesusüberlieferungen', in G. Dautzenberg, H. Merklein and K. Müller (eds), *Die Frau im Urchristentum*, Freiburg 1983, 9-91 (the book also contains contributions on the mother of Jesus and on women as witnesses to Easter); B. Witherington, *Women in the Ministry of Jesus. A Study of Jesus' Attitudes to Women and their Roles as reflected in His Earthly Life*, Cambridge 1984.

4.  Luke 10.38–42; John 11.3, 5, 28f., 36.

5.  Cf. Mark 3.1–4.

6.  Cf. I Cor. 15.5–7.

7.  Mark 15.20f. par.; 15.47 par.

8.  Cf. Mark 3.31–35 par.; 10.29f. par.

9.  Luke 16.18.

10. Cf. I Cor. 7. Cf. the contribution by H. Merklein in Chapter VII of *Die Frau im Urchristentum* (n.3).

11. E. Schüssler Fiorenza, *In Memory of Her. A Feminist Theological Reconstruction of Christian Origins*, London and New York 1983, 135f.

12. Ibid., 138. For the limits to the 'argument from silence' cf. the critical comments by S. Heine, 'Brille der Parteilichkeit. Zu einer feministischen Hermeneutik', *Evangelische Kommentare* 23, 1990, 354–7.

13. Schüssler Fiorenza, *In Memory of Her* (n.11), 186.
14. Ead., 140.
15. Ead., 121.
16. Luke 4.32.
17. Acts 21.9.
18. Mark 9.35; 10.43 par.

## 2. Women in the Early Church

1. Cf. E. Käsemann, 'Ministry and Community in the New Testament', in *Essays on New Testament Themes*, London 1964, 63–92. For charisms see further M. Hengel, *Nachfolge und Charisma. Eine exegetisch-religionsgeschichtliche Studie zu Mt 8, 21f. und Jesu Ruf in die Nachfolge*, Vienna 1968; G. Hasenhüttl, *Charisma. Ordnungsprinzip der Kirche*, Freiburg 1969; U. Brockhaus, *Charisma und Amt. Die paulinischer Charismenlehre auf dem Hintergrund der frühchristlichen Gemeindefunktion*, Wuppertal 1972; J. Hainz, *Ekklesia – Strukturen paulinische Gemeinde-Theologie und Gemeinde-Ordnung*, Regensburg 1972.

2. Gal. 3.27f. There is already a 90-page bibliography on the question of women in the New Testament: I. M. Lindbøe, *Women in the New Testament. A Select Bibliography*, Oslo 1990. In addition to E. Schüssler Fiorenza, *In Memory of Her*, New York and London 1983, which I have already cited several times, cf. above all O. Bangerter, *Frauen im Aufbruch. Die Geschichte einer Frauenbewegung in der alten Kirche. Ein Beitrag zur Frauenfrage*, Neukirchen 1971; E. M. Tetlow, *Women and Ministry in the New Testament*, New York 1980; R. Rieplhuber, *Die Stellung der Frau in den neutestamentlichen Schriften und im Koran*, Altenberge 1986; B. Witherington, *Women in the Earliest Churches*, Cambridge 1988; id., *Women and the Genesis of Christianity*, Cambridge 1990; B. Bowman Thurston, *The*

*Widows. A Women's Ministry in the Early Church*, Minneapolis 1989; N. Baumert, *Antifeminismus bei Paulus? Einzelstudien*, Würzburg 1992; id., *Frau und Mann bei Paulus. Überwindung eines Missverständnisses*, Würzburg 1992; C. S. Keener, *Paul, Women and Wives. Marriage and Women's Ministry in the Letters of Paul*, Peabody, Mass. 1992.

3. Cf. Rom. 16.1–16.
4. For the titles *diakonos* and *prostatis* cf. Schüssler Fiorenza, *In Memory of Her* (n.2), 170–2.
5. Cf. Rom. 16.7.
6. U. Wilckens, *Der Brief an die Römer*, Vol. III, Zurich 1982, 135.
7. Cf. I Thess. 5.12; Rom. 16.6,12.
8. Phil. 4.2f.
9. Cf. Rom. 16.3; I Cor. 16.19; Acts 18.1; 18.18f.; 18.26.
10. Cf. I Cor. 1 6.19; II Tim. 4.19.
11. I Cor. 11.5.
12. Eph. 2.20.
13. Schüssler Fiorenza, *In Memory of Her* (n.2), 183.
14. Cf. M. Küchler, *Schweigen, Schmuck und Schleier. Drei neutestamentlichen Vorschriften zur Verdrängung der Frauen auf dem Hintergrund einer frauenfeindlichen Exegese des Alten Testaments im antiken Judentum*, Fribourg 1986.
15. Cf. I Cor. 11.3.
16. Cf. I Cor. 14.34f.
17. I Tim. 2.11f.
18. Cf. Rom. 16.7. B. Brooten, '"Junia . . . hervorragend unter den Aposteln" (Rom. 16.7)', in E. Moltmann-Wendel (ed.), *Frauenbefreiung. Biblische und theologische Argumente*, Munich 1978, 148–51, has made a detailed investigation of this. V. Fabrega, 'War Junia(s), der hervorragende Apostel (Rom 16,7), eine Frau?', *Jahrbuch für Antike und Christentum* 27/28, 1984/5, 47–64. Of the more recent

commentaries on Romans, that by U. Wilckens has been open to the arguments advanced here (135).

19. Cf. R. Albrecht, *Das Leben der heiligen Makrina auf dem Hintergrund der Thekla-Traditionen. Studien zu den Ursprüngen des weiblichen Mönchtums im vierten Jahrhundert in Kleinasien*, Göttingen 1986, ch. 5. A. Jensen (ed.), *Thekla die Apostolin – Ein apokrypher Text neu entdeckt*, Freiburg 1995.

20. Cf. John 19.25–27.

21. Cf. Mark 16.9–11; John 20.11–18.

22. Cf. E. Moltmann-Wendel, *The Women around Jesus*, London and New York 1982, ch. 3, 'Mary Magdalene'.

23. For the role of women in the sphere of Gnosticism cf. A. Jensen, *Gottes selbstbewusste Töchter. Frauenemanzipation im frühen Christentum?*, Freiburg 1992, 367–71.

24. Cf. W. Bauer, *Orthodoxy and Heresy in Earliest Christianity* (1934), Philadelphia and London 1972.

25. The fair historical monograph by A. von Harnack, *Marcion. Das Evangelium vom fremden Gott* (1920), is still a model today. It is published, with an appendix, in *Neue Studien zu Marcion*, Darmstadt ³1960. More recent monographs have been written by J. Knox, *Marcion and the New Testament. An Essay in the Early History of the Canon*, Chicago 1942; E. C. Blackman, *Marcion and His Influence*, London 1948. Cf. also the brief summary by K. Beyschlag, 'Marcion von Sinope', in *Gestalten der Kirchengeschichte*, Stuttgart 1984, 69–81.

26. These works by Perpetua, Proba, Egeria and Eudokia have now been collected in one volume with introductions and notes by P. Wilson-Kästner et al. (eds), *A Lost Tradition. Women Writers of the Early Church*, Washington 1981.

27. K. Thraede, 'Frau', in *Reallexikon für Antike und Christentum* VIII, Stuttgart 1972, 197–269: 240f. For women in antiquity including early Christianity cf. G. Duby and M. Perrot (eds), *Storia delle donne in occidente* 1 (ed. P.

Schmitt Pantel), Rome 1990 (which contains a fine survey of women in early Christianity by M. Alexandre).

28. At the Institute for Ecumenical Research of Tübingen University, under my direction and with advice from Dr Elisabeth Moltmann-Wendel, a research project was undertaken on 'Women and Christianity', generously supported by the Volkswagen Foundation. It consisted of two part-projects, 'Sexuality, Marriage and Alternatives to Marriage in the First Four Christian Centuries' (under Dr Anne Jensen), and 'Being a Christian Woman in Twentieth-Century Church and Society' (under Dr Doris Kaufmann). The results of the research were published in two monographs: D. Kaufmann, *Frauen zwischen Aufbruch und Reaktion. Protestantische Frauenbewegung in der ersten Hälfte des 2.Jahrhunderts*, Munich 1988; A. Jensen, *Gottes selbstbewusste Töchter. Frauenemanzipation im frühen Christentum?*, Freiburg 1992.

29. A. von Harnack, *The Expansion of Christianity in the First Three Centuries*, London 1904–5, II, 217–39, and the work of his pupil, L. Zscharnack, *Der Dienst der Frau in den ersten Jahrhunderten der christlichen Kirche*, Göttingen 1902, are still basic studies of the role of women in early Christianity. In this connection reference should be made to the important works (details are given in the bibliography of A. Jensen's monograph, n. 28) on the ordination of women in the early church (R. Gryson) or the refusal of ordination (I. Raming), and to the 'collections of sources' now available in different languages about the role of women in early Christianity (O. Bangerter, J. Beaucamp, M. Ibarta Benlloch, J. Laporte, C. Mazzucco, C. Militello, S. Tunc) and to the pioneering work of American feminists (E. Castelli, E. Clark, R. Kraemer, J. A. McNamara, R. Ruether).

30. Cf. Jensen, *Gottes selbstbewussteTöchter* (n. 28), ch. 1, 'Frauen in den Kirchengeschichten: Die Entwicklung zur Männerkirche'.

31. Cf. ibid., ch. II, 'Frauen im Martyrium . . . Mutige Bekennerinnen'.
32. Cf. ibid., ch. III, 'Frauen in der Verkündigung: Charismatische Prophetinnen'.
33. Cf. ibid., ch. IV, 'Erlösung durch Erkenntnis. Kluge Lehrerinnen'.
34. Thraede, 'Frau' (n. 27), 244f.
35. Peter Brown, 'Antiquité tardive', in P. Ariès and G. Duby, *Histoire de la vie privée*, I, Paris 1985, 265. Cf. id., *The Making of Late Antiquity*, Cambridge, Mass. 1978.

## 3. Women in the Church of the Middle Ages

1. Augustine, *In primam epistolam Ioannis* VII.8. Cf. D. Dideberg, *Saint Augustin et la première épître de saint Jean. Une théologie de l'agape*, Paris 1975.
2. Cf. Augustine, *De nuptiis et concupiscentia* 1, 24f.
3. Cf. K. E. Børresen, *Subordination et Equivalence. Nature et rôle de la femme d'après Augustin et Thomas d'Aquin*, Oslo 1968, esp. ch. I, 1-3.
4. For Augustine's attitude to sexuality before and after his conversion cf. P. Brown, *The Body and Society. Men, Women and Sexual Renunciation in Early Christianity*, London and New York 1988, 406–27. Augustine's theory of sex and sin was so important to him that at the age of 70 he sent a letter to Patriarch Atticus of Constantinople, John Chrysostom's successor (it has only been recently discovered), summing up his position as follows: 'An urge (he means the evil 'urge of the flesh') which burns quite indiscriminately for objects allowed and disallowed; and which is bridled by the urge for marriage (*concupiscentia nuptiarum*), that must depend on it, but that restrains it from what is not allowed . . . Against this drive, which is in tension with the law of the mind, all chastity must fight: that of the married couple, so that the urge of the flesh may

be rightly used, and that of continent men and virgins. So that, even better, and with a struggle of greater glory, it should not be used at all. This urge, had it existed in Paradise . . . would, in a wondrous height of peace, never have run beyond the bidding of the will . . . It would never have forced itself upon the mind with thoughts of inappropriate and impermissible delights. It would not have had to be held upon the leash by married moderation, nor fought to a draw by ascetic labour. Rather, when once called for, it would have followed the will of the person with all the case of a single-hearted act of obedience' (quoted in Brown, *The Body and Society*, 423).

5. J. G. Ziegler, *Die Ehelehre der Pönitentialsummen von 1200–1350. Eine Untersuchung zur Geschichte der Moral- und Pastoraltheologie*, Regensburg 1956, 169.

6. For what follows see the summary of historical research in A. Angenendt, *Das Frühmittelalter. Die abendlandische Christenheit von 400 bis 900*, Stuttgart 1990, 345f. There is much material on the restrictions on the consummation of marriage and the demonization of the sexual in Ziegler, *Ehelehre* (n. 5), Part IV.

7. For criticism of these views from the Catholic side see S. H. Pfürtner, *Kirche und Sexualitit*, Hamburg 1972; id., *Sexualfeindschaft und Macht. Eine Streitschrift für verantwortete Freiheit in der Kirche*, Mainz 1992; G. Denzler, *Die verbotene Lust. 200 Jahre christliche Sexualmoral*, Munich 1988.

8. Thus already during the Second Vatican Council the Viennese pastoral theologian M. Pfliegler summed up the German petition in a critical forerunner to the post-conciliar Catholic critiques of celibacy, *Der Zölibat*, which I included in the series Theologische Meditationen, Einsiedeln 1965; this was then followed by a whole series of books criticizing celibacy, including those of F. Leist (1968) and A. Antweiler (1969). The standard historical

work on the question was written by the Catholic church historian from Bamberg, G. Denzler, *Das Papsttum und der Amtszölibat*, I–II, Stuttgart 1973/76, short version *Die Geschichte des Zölibats*, Freiburg 1993. This work not only quotes the church documents enforcing celibacy on the clergy in connection with the Gregorian reform, but also shows the tremendous discrimination against the wives of priests, who were still legitimate at the time; one needs only to read the taunts of Peter Damian (58–62), which may be said to be pathological, also to have a better understanding of the political agitation of his fellow cardinal, who later became Pope Gregory VII (64–74). But the countless testimonies to the resistance of the clergy to the pope and the initially few bishops loyal to Rome, a resistance which was quite general in Germany but ultimately unsuccessful, is also important. Cf. also A. L. Barstow, *Married Priests and the Reforming Papacy. The Eleventh-Century Debates*, New York 1982. For the further context cf. Denzler, *Die verbotene Lust* (n. 7).

9. Cf. Thomas Aquinas, *Summa theologiae*, I, q.92, a.1–4.
10. Cf. ibid., II–II, q.177, a.2. A. Mitterer, 'Mann und Weib nach dem biologischen Weltbild des hl.Thomas und dem der Gegenwart', *Zeitschrift für katholische Theologie* 57, 1933, 491–556; id., *Die Zeugung der Organismen, insbesondere des Menschen, nach dem Weltbild des hl.Thomas von Aquin und dem der Gegenwart*, Vienna 1947, already drew attention to Thomas' androcentrism and the way in which he often regards the woman as inferior.
11. Cf. Thomas Aquinas, *Summa theologiae*, I, q.92, a.1.
12. For *occasionatus*, A. Blaise (ed.), *Lexicon latinitatis medii aevi*, Turnhout 1975, has '1. causé occasionellement, 2. imparfait, manqué'. Cf. also A. Mitterer, 'Mas occasionatus oder zwei Methoden der Thomasdeutung', *Zeitschrift für katholische Theologie* 72, 1950, 80–103.

13. Cf. Thomas Aquinas, *Commentary on the Sentences*, IV, d.25, q.2. qla 1, ad 4.
14. Cf. id., *Summa theologiae*, Supplementum, q.39, a.1.
15. At that time lay preaching was in any case a particularly provocative theme in view of the heretical movements. Thomas even explicitly opposes an office of preaching and teaching for women, a 'grace of the discourse of wisdom and science', used by them *publice*, and does so with special arguments (cf. *Summa theologiae*, II–II, q.177, a.2):
    - Above all because of the condition that the female sex shall be subject to the man: teaching as a public office in the church is a matter for those set in authority (*praelati*) and not for subjects; these essentially include the woman because of her sex (and thus not just accidentally, like the simple priest, who is at any rate male);
    - Also for the sake of males, whose senses are not to be stimulated to lust by preaching women (lust = *concupiscentia* or *libido* has been a widespread theme since Augustine!);
    - Finally, women in any case would not distinguish themselves in matters of wisdom to such a degree that they could be entrusted with a public task of teaching.
16. Cf. K. E. Børresen, *Subordination and Equivalence. The Nature and Role of Woman in Augustine and Thomas Aquinas*, Washington 1981; ead., 'Die anthropologischen Grundlagen der Beziehung zwischen Mann und Frau in der klassischen Theologie', *Concilium* 12, 1976, 10–17 (never translated into English); ead., *Image of God and Gender Models in Judaeo–Christian Tradition*, Oslo 1991; K. E. Børresen and K. Vogt, *Women's Studies of the Christian and Islamic Traditions. Ancient, Medieval and Renaissance Foremothers*, Dordrecht 1993. I am deeply grateful to Dr Kari Børresen of the University of Oslo for looking through the present book and for her valuable suggestions.

17. According to Børresen, too, there are significant differences between Augustine and Thomas over women. It is not just that Augustine gets by without a precise physiological theory and Thomas explicitly builds on the physiology of Aristotle, who is responsible for his remarkable statements about women. In addition, because of his less pessimistic attitude to the reality of creation, Thomas has a more positive attitude to sexuality throughout.

   - Unlike Augustine, Thomas does not advocate a dualistic anthropology even for the original reality of creation (in paradise). The sensual feelings of the body are an essential part of human beings, and under the conditions of 'paradise' there could have been sexual intercourse even without sin: 'Consequently the natural satisfaction, as it would have been wholly governed by the reason, would have been even greater than the pleasure which is now associated with the sexual act' (Børresen, 'Die anthropologische Grundlagen' [n.16], 12, referring to *Summa theologiae* I, q. 98, a.1, 2).

   - Unlike Augustine, Thomas has no almost compulsive anxiety about a sexuality allegedly corrupted by original sin and its irrational character. He avoids the Augustinian identification of original sin with sexual desire (*concupiscentia, libido*): 'He breaks with this tradition in distinguishing between procreation (in which the father's seed works as an instrumental cause in passing on original sin) and desire, which normally accompanies sexual intercourse, but which does not represent any causal factor' (13, with reference to *Summa theologiae* I–II, q.82, a.3; q.85, a.1).

   - Unlike Augustine, Thomas does not simply see sexuality and its disorderly desire justified in marriage by the benefit of fertility (as though the ideal married love consisted in a continent love): 'Not only the intention of fertility but also the use of marriage as a means of salvation (from concupiscence) make the sexual act free from sin' (15, with reference to *Summa theologiae*, Supplementum q.41, a.3; q.42, a.2; q.49, a.5).

J. B. Bauer draws my attention to Thomas' insistence on the *ligatio rationis in concubitu conjugali: Summa theologiae*, I–II, q.34, a.1 ad 1; q.37, a1. ad 2; q.72, a.2 ad 4; II–II, q.150, a.4 ad 3; q.153, a.2.

18. For women in the Middle Ages cf. T. Vogelsang, *Die Frau als Herrscherin im hohen Mittelalter. Studien zur 'consors regni' Formel*, Göttingen 1954; M. Bernards, *Speculum virginum. Geistigkeit und Seelenleben der Frau im Hochmittelalter*, Cologne 1955; G. Koch, *Frauenfrage und Ketzertum im Mittelalter. Die Frauenbewegung im Rahmen des Katharismus und des Waldensertums und ihre sozialen Wurzeln (12–14 Jahrhundert)*, Berlin 1962; I. Raming, *Der Auschluss der Frau vom priesterlichen Amt. Gottgewollte Tradition oder Diskriminierung? Eine rechtshistorisch-dogmatische Untersuchung der Grundlagen von Kanon 968 I des Codex Iuris Canonici*, Cologne 1973; J. M. Ferrante, *Woman as Image in Mediaeval Literature from the Twelfth Century to Dante*, New York 1975; E. Power, *Medieval Women*, Cambridge 1975; M. Bogin, *The Women Troubadours*, New York 1976; B. A. Carroll (ed.), *Liberating Women's History. Theoretical and Critical Essays*, Urbana 1976; F. and J. Cies, *Women in the Middle Ages*, New York 1978; A. Wolf-Graaf, *Frauenarbeit im Abseits. Frauenbewegung und weibliches Arbeitsvermögen*, Munich 1981; A. Kuhn and J. Rüsen (eds), *Frauen in der Geschichte* II, Düsseldorf 1982f.; P. Ketsch, *Frauen im Mittelalter. Quellen und Materialien, I, Frauenarbeit im Mittelalter; II, Frauenbild und Frauenrechte im Kirche und Gesellschaft*, Düsseldorf 1983; A. M. Lucas, *Women in the Middle Ages. Religion, Marriage and Letters*, Brighton 1983; I. Ludolphy, 'Frau' (V). Alte Kirche und Mittelalter', *TRE* XI, 436–41; E. Ennen, *Frauen im Mittelalter*, Munich

1984, ⁴1991; D. Herlihy, *Mediaeval Households*, Cambridge, Mass. 1935; M. C. Howell, *Women, Production and Patriarchy in Late Medieval Cities*, Chicago 1986; M. B. Rose (ed.), *Women in the Middle Ages and the Renaissance. Literary and Historical Perspectives*, Syracuse 1986; B. Frakele, E. List and G. Pauritsch (eds), *Über Frauenleben, Männerwelt und Wissenschaft. Österreichische Texte zur Frauenforschung*, Vienna 1987; A. Kuhn, 'Mittelalter', in *Frauenlexikon. Traditionen, Fakten, Perspektiven*, ed. A. Lossner, R. Süssmuth and K. Walter, Freiburg 1988, 749–60; S. Shahar, *Die Frau im Mittelalter*, Königstein 1988; F. Bertini et al., *Medioevo al femminile*, Bari 1989; G. Duby and M. Perrot, *Storia delle donne in occidente*, Vol. II (ed. C. Klapisch-Zuber), Rome 1990; J. B. Holloway, C. S. Wright and J. Bechtold (eds), *Equally in God's Image. Women in the Middle Ages*, New York 1990; C. Opitz, *Evatöchter und Bruder Christi. Weiblicher Lebenszusammenhang und Frauenkultur im Mittelalter*, Weinheim 1990; C. Walker Bynum, *Fragmentation and Redemption. Essays on Gender and the Human Body in Mediaeval Religion*, New York 1991; B. Lundt (ed.), *Auf der Suche nach der Frau im Mittelalter. Fragen, Quellen, Antworten*, Munich 1991; R. Pernoud, *Leben der Frauen im Hochmittelalter* (there is a French original), Pfaffenweiler 1991; Borresen and Vogt, *Women's Studies* (n. 16, the survey of research by K. E. Børresen on pp. 13-127, is particularly important here). The collection of sources edited by E. Gössmann, *Archiv für philosophie- und theologiegeschichtliche Frauenforschung* (8 vols so far), Munich 1984–95, is especially worthwhile.

19. Cf. Chapter II above, 'Were women emancipated through Christianity?'

20. Cf. Chapter III above, 'Rigorism in sexual morality'.

21. J. Le Goff, *L'imaginaire médiaeval*, Paris 1985, 123.

22. One wonders, for example, what was the specific signi-

ficance of the 'guardianship' under which women were put at that time, simply by virtue of their sex. What did this sexual supervision, first by the father and then by the husband, mean? Did it leave the women any legal rights and freedom of action? And what about a special Germanic form of marriage like 'Friedelehe', without a dowry, in which the husband had no mastery over his wife? What was the position among the Langobards (and perhaps also among the Franks and Anglo-Saxons)? Were women there still unable to administer, use and increase their property independently in the seventh century? Indeed, didn't a partnership between husband and wife predominate in the peasant households of the Middle Ages, so that a verdict is difficult because on the basis of the predominantly male sources we have better knowledge about the legal position of women in the Middle Ages than about their social status?

23. Ennen, *Frauen im Mittelalter* (n. 18), 108.
24. Ibid.
25. Kuhn, 'Mittelalter' (n.18), 753f.
26. Cf. Howell, *Women* (n.18).
27. Kuhn, 'Mittelalter' (n.18), 758f.
28. Cf. Giorgio Tourn, *Geschichte der Waldenser-Kirche*, Kassel and Erlangen 1980, 18.
29. Cf. U. Baumann, *Die Ehe – ein Sakrament?*, Zurich 1988.
30. Cf. R. Kieckhefer, *Repression of Heresy in Medieval Germany*, Philadelphia 1979, ch. 3, 'The War against Beghards and Beguines'. P. D. Johnson, *Equal in Monastic Profession. Religious Women in Medieval France*, Chicago 1991, notes a collapse in women's monastic culture from the twelfth century on.
31. Ennen, *Frauen im Mittelalter* (n.18), 245; cf. M. Schmidt and K. E. Børresen, 'Theologin (I-II)', in E. Gössmann et al. (eds), *Wörterbuch der Feministischen Theologie*, Gütersloh 1991, 396-415.

32. Cf. the portrait by E. Gössmann, 'Hildegard von Bingen', in M. Greschat (ed.), *Gestalten der Kirchengeschichte* III, 224-37 (with bibliography).

33. For mysticism, cf. in addition to earlier works which are still important (above all the reprints of books by C. Butler, J. Bernhart and W. Preger): L. Bouyer et al. (eds), *Histoire de la spiritualité chrétienne* (3 vols), Paris 1960–66; K. Ruh (ed.), *Altdeutsche und altniederländische Mystik*, Darmstadt 1944; id., *Geschichte der abendländischen Mystik* (2 vols), Munich 1990/93; L. Cognet, *Introduction aux mystiques rhéno-flamands*, Paris 1968; F. W. Wentzlaff-Eggebert, *Deutsche Mystik zwischen Mittelalter und Neuzeit. Einheit und Wandlung ihrer Erscheinungsformen*, Berlin ³1969; A. M. Haas and H. Stirnimann, *Das 'Einig Ein'. Studien zu Theorie und Sprache der deutschen Mystik*, Fribourg 1980; J. Sudbrack (ed.), *Zeugen christlicher Gotteserfahrung*, Mainz 1981; id., *Mystik. Selbsterfahrung – kosmische Erfahrung – Gotteserfahrung*, Mainz 1988; G. Ruhbach and J. Sudbrack (eds), *Grosse Mystiker. Leben und Wirken*, Munich 1987; id. (ed.), *Christliche Mystik. Texte aus zwei Jahrtausenden*, Munich 1989; R. Beyer, *Die andere Offenbarungen. Mystikerinnen des Mittelalters*, Bergisch-Gladbach 1989; B. McGinn, *The Foundations of Mysticism*, London and New York 1991; P. Dinzelbacher, *Mittelalterliche Frauenmystik*, Paderborn 1993.

34. Cf. K. Ruh, 'Le miroir des simples âmes de Marguerite Porete' (1975), in *Kleine Schriften* II, Berlin 1984, 212–36; id., *Meister Eckhart, Theologe, Prediger, Mystiker*, Munich 1985, 95–114.

35. Cf. E. Gössmann, 'Die Geschichte und Lehre der Mystikerin Marguerite Porete (gest.1310)', in Hiring and Kuschel (eds), *Gegenentwürfe*, 69–79. Cf. further works on Porete in Børresen and Vogt, *Women's Studies* (n.16), 70–2.

36. For the history of the veneration of Mary cf. G. Miegge, *The*

*Virgin Mary*, London 1955; W. Tappolet (ed.), *Das Marien-lob der Reformatoren. M. Luther, J. Calvin, H. Zwingli, H. Bullinger*, Tübingen 1962; W. Delius, *Geschichte der Marienverehrung*, Munich 1963; H. Graef, *Maria. Eine Geschichte der Lehre und Verehrung*, Freiburg 1964.

37. Cf. Denzinger, *Enchiridion*, no.111a; G. Galbiati, *Il Concilio di Efeso. Alle origini dei dogmi e del culto di Maria nel tormentato clima del Concilio di Efeso, tappa miliare per l'avento della mariologia*, Genoa 1977; S. Benko, *The Virgin Goddess. Studies in the Pagan and Christian Roots of Mariology*, Leiden 1993.

38. Cf. K.-J. Kuschel (ed.), *Und Maria trat aus ihren Bildern. Literarische Texte*, Freiburg 1990.

39. For the lack of biblical foundations for Marian dogmas cf. the article by the American Catholic exegete J. McKenzie, 'Die Mutter Jesu im Neuen Testament', in E. Moltmann-Wendel, H. Küng and J. Moltmann (eds), *Was geht uns Maria an? Beiträge zur Auseinandersetzung in Theologie, Kirche und Frömmigkeit*, Gütersloh 1988, 233–40. K. E. Børresen, 'Maria in der katholischen Theologie', demonstrates that the two more recent dogmatic formulations about Mary are based on 'wrong anthropological presuppositions' (ibid., 72–87). This specialist in the history of dogma and theology puts forward 'the theory that these formulations lose their meaning and become literally incomprehensible as soon as their a prioris are no longer retained. If these mariocentric statements are no longer supported by the Augustinian doctrine of original sin handed down through the father's procreation or the classical doctrine of the immortal rational soul separate from the body, with its expectation of the risen body, they remain suspended in the void of sheer conjecture' (81). The volume mentioned above also contains contributions by internationally recognized professionals from Jewish and feminist, critical and traditional perspectives, quoted

below, which give a survey of the state of present-day discussion on Mary.

40. C. J. M. Halkes, 'Maria – inspirierendes oder abschrek-
    kendes Vorbild für Frauen?', in Moltmann-Wendel et al.
    (eds), *Was geht uns Maria an?* (n. 38), 113–30: 114.

41. Cf. E. Drewermann, *Kleriker. Psychogramm eines Ideals*,
    Freiburg 1989, esp. 11 B 2 d.

42. J. Moltmann, 'Gibt es eine ökumenische Mariologie?', in
    Moltmann-Wendel et al. (eds), *Was geht uns Maria an?* (n.
    38), 15–22: 15; cf. here also S. Ben-Chorin, *Die Mutter Jesu
    in jüdischer Sicht*, 40–50.

43. Luke 1.48.

44. Cf. Mark 3.20f.

45. For the biblical evidence, in addition to the article by J.
    McKenzie cited above see the joint study by Protestant and
    Roman Catholic scholars: R. E. Brown, K. P. Donfried, J. A.
    Fitzmyer and J. Reumann (eds), *Mary in the New Testa-
    ment. A Collaborative Assessment by Protestant and
    Roman Catholic Scholars*, Philadelphia 1978.

46. Cf. M. Warner, *Alone of All Her Sex. The Myth and the Cult
    of the Virgin Mary*, London 1976.

47. Halkes, 'Maria' (n.18), rightly attaches importance to this
    from the feminist perspective.

48. For the question of the virgin birth cf. H. Küng, *Credo*,
    London and New York 1993, ch. II, 'Jesus Christ; Virgin
    Birth and Divine Sonship'. For the question of the pre-
    existence of Christ see K-J. Kuschel, *Born Before All Time?
    The Dispute over Christ's Origin*, London and New York
    1992.

49. Cf. Luke 1.38; 2.34f.

50. Luke 1.

51. However, the New Testament does not once hint at a lover
    or even a wife of Jesus – the material for novels, musicals
    and writers of trivia; quite the contrary. Elisabeth
    Moltmann-Wendel (Tübingen) rightly highlights the

repressed tradition of Jesus' friendship with Mary Magdalene over against the excessive stress on that of Jesus' mother Mary. I am grateful to her for a number of suggestions; she championed feminist concerns critically and constructively in the German-speaking world, earlier than others. See her 'Maria oder Magdalena – Mutterschaft oder Freundschaft', in ead., *Was geht uns Maria an?* (n. 38), 51-9.

52. Gal. 5.1.
53. II Cor. 3.17.
54. Gal. 3.27f.

## 4. Women at the Time of the Reformation

1. U. Baumann, *Die Ehe – ein Sakrament?*, Zurich 1988, 29–44, esp. 33f., is right in his interpretation here.
2. G. Scharffenorth, 'Im Geiste Freunde werden . . . Die Beziehung von Mann und Frau bei Luther im Rahmen seines Kirchenverständnisses', in ead., *Die Glauben ins Leben ziehen . . . Studien zu Luthers Theologie*, Munich 1982, 122–202: 164.
3. Ibid., 174.
4. Ibid., 162.
5. Luther, 'Welche Personen verboten sind zu ehelichen' (1522), WA X/2, 263–6: 266.
6. Cf. id., 'To the Councilmen of All Cities in Germany, that they Establish and Maintain Christian Schools', LW 45, 341–78.
7. Cf. E. Reichle, 'Reformation', in A. Lissner, R. Süssmuth and K. Walter (eds), *Frauenlexikon. Traditionen, Fakten, Perspektiven*, Freiburg 1988, 927–34; R. H. Bainton, *Women of the Reformation*, Vol. I, *In Germany and Italy*; Vol. II, *In France and England*; Vol. III, *From Spain to Scandinavia*, Minneapolis 1971–77, investigates the question in the European context.

8. Cf. Ch. III, 'Women in the family, politics and business'.
9. Cf. I. Ludolphy, 'Frau (VI. Reformationszeit)', *TRE* XI, 441–3; S. E. Ozment, *When Fathers Ruled. Family Life in Reformation Europe*, Cambridge, Mass. 1983; L. Roper, *The Holy Household. Women and Morals in Reformation Augsburg*, Oxford 1989.
10. Cf. J. Dempsey Douglass, *Women, Freedom, and Calvin*, Philadelphia 1985.
11. Cf. R. L. Greaves (ed.), *Triumph over Silence. Women in Protestant History*, London 1985.
12. Cf. P. Crawford, *Women and Religion in England 1500–1720*, London 1993.
13. Cf. M. P. Hannay, *Silent but for the Word. Tudor Women as Patrons, Translators and Writers of Religious Works*, Kent 1985.
14. Crawford (n.12) devotes a whole chapter to them.
15. Cf. M. Kobelt-Groch, *Aufsässige Töchter Gottes. Frauen im Bauernkrieg und in den Täuferbewegungen*, Frankfurt 1993.
16. Cf. the evaluation by the Catholic theologian A. Jensen, 'Im Kampf um Freiheit in Kirche und Staat: Die Mutter des Quäkertums, Margaret Fell', in H. Häring and K.-J. Kuschel (eds), *Gegenentwürfe. 24 Lebensläufe für eine andere Theologie*, Munich 1988, 169–80.
17. Crawford, *Women and Religion* (n.12),138.
18. Ibid., 139.
19. Ibid.
20. Greaves (ed.), *Triumph over Silence* (n.11), 12.
21. There are already numerous detailed investigations of the persecution of witches in particular regions (B. Ankarloo, Sweden; G. Bader, Switzerland; W. Behringer, south-east Germany; G. Bonomo, Italy; F. Byloff, Austria; P. F. Byrne, Ireland; G. Henningsen, Basque country; C. Larner, Scotland; A. Macfarlane, England; R. Mandrou, France; H. C. E. Midelfort, south-west Germany; E. W. Monter, France

and Switzerland; J. Tazbir, Poland; R. Zguta, Russia). For Germany there is a survey of research by G. Schormann, *Hexenprozesse in Deutschland*, Göttingen 1981 (the same author has also written an admirable survey, 'Hexen', *TRE* XV, 297–304); cf. also the informative documentation by W. Behringer (ed.), *Hexen und Hexenprozesse in Deutschland*, Munich 1988, 1933. Further more recent literature on this topic includes: N. C. Cohn, *Europe's Inner Demons. An Enquiry Inspired by the Great Witch-Hunt*, London 1975; R. Kieckhefer, *European Witch Trials. Their Foundations in Popular and Learned Culture, 1300–1500*, London 1976; H. Döbler, *Hexenwahn. Die Geschichte einer Verfolgung*, Munich 1977; M. Hammes, *Hexenwahn und Hexenprozesse*, Frankfurt 1977; C. Honegger (ed.), *Die Hexen der Neuzeit. Studien zur Sozialgeschichte eines kulturellen Deutungsmusters*, Frankfurt 1978; C. Ginzburg, *I Benandanti. Stregoneria e culti agrari tra Cinquecento e Seicento*, Turin 1966; E. Wissenlinck, *Hexen. Warum wir so wenig von ihrer Geschicbte erfahren und was davon auch noch falsch ist*, Munich 1986; R. van Dülmen (ed.), *Hexenwelten. Magie und Imagination vom 16.–20. Jahrhundert*, Frankfurt 1987; G. Schwaiger (ed.), *Teufelsglaube und Hexenprozesse*, Munich 1987; H. Weber, *Kinderhexenprozesse*, Frankfurt 1991.

22. H. Haag, *Vor dem Bösen Ratlos?*, Munich 1978, 164; cf. also id. and K. Elliger, *Teufelsglaube*, Tübingen 1974, ch. 4, 'Die Hexen'.

23. Cf. e.g. Thomas Aquinas, *Summa theologiae* II-II, q.93, a.2.

24. Cf. J. Sprenger and H. Institoris, *Malleus maleficarum* (1487); for the first time translated into German (in three parts) with an introduction by J. W. R. Schmidt, Berlin 1906, reprinted 1974. That the obscenities and perversions of which the witches were accused were to some degree a substitute satisfaction of sexual desires forbidden to Christians (and especially celibate priests) is not only a

psychologizing hypothesis but is clearly demonstrated in this book: page after page there are discussions of 'whether witches can prevent the power to beget or the enjoyment of love' (1, 127–36), or 'whether witches bewitch male members by false illusions' (1, 136–45), and many examples are given 'of the manner in which they used to bewitch away male members' (11, 78–87).

25. The original Latin text of the bull is to be found in C. Mirbt and K. Aland, *Quellen zur Geschichte des Papsttums und des römischen Katholizismus* I, Tübingen ⁶1967, 282f.

26. Schormann, 'Hexen' (n. 21), 303.

27. C. Honegger, 'Hexen', in A. Lissner, R. Süssmuth and K. Walter (eds), *Frauenlexikon. Traditionen, Fakten, Perspektiven*, Freiburg 1988, 491–500: 498.

28. Cf. F. von Spee, *Cautio criminalis, seu de processibus contra sagas* (1631); German edition: *Cautio criminalis oder Rechtliche Bedenken wegen der Hexenprozesse*, Weimar 1939.

## 5. Women in Modernity and Postmodernity

1. Cf. I. Kant, 'Beobachtungen über das Gefühl des Schönen und Erhabenen' (1764), in *Werke* I, 821-84: 851f.

2. Cf. J. J. Bachofen, *Das Mutterrecht. Eine Untersuchung über die Gynaikokratie der alten Welt nach ihrer religiösen und rechtlichen Natur*, Stuttgart 1861.

3. 'Declaration of the Rights of Women and Citizenesses', text in H. Schröder and T. Sauter, 'Zur politischen Theorie des Feminismus. Die Deklaration der Rechte der Frau und Bürgerin von 1791', in *Aus Politik und Zeitgeschichte*, supplement to the weekly *Das Parliament* 48, 1977, 29–54: 51. Cf. L. Doormann, *Ein Feuer brennt in mir. Die Lebensgeschichte der Olympe de Gouges*, Weinheim 1993.

4. Marx and Engels, *The Communist Manifesto*, London 1988, reissued Harmondsworth 1967, 101.

5. Cf. F. Engels, *The Origin of the Family, Private Property and the State* (1884), Harmondsworth 1986.

6. Cf. A. Bebel, *Woman in the Past, Present and Future* (1879), London 1988.

7. As late as 1931 'the corporate order' was still the main value of Pius XI's second social encyclical *Quadragesimo Anno* (= 40 years after *Rerum novarum*). There were attempts to realize a corporative state in Austria between 1934 and 1938 and corporative chambers in Portugal, Spain and Italy.

8. M. Greschat, *Das Zeitalter der Industriellen Revolution. Das Christentum vor der Moderne*, Stuttgart 1980, 236.

9. Leo XIII, Encyclical *Immortale Dei* (1885), in E. Marmu (ed.), *Mensch und Gemeinschaft*, nos 833–907: 867.

10. Leo XIII, Encyclical *Rerum novarum*, Centenary Edition, London 1992, §42.

11. S. H. Pfürtner, 'Soziallehre, katholische', in *Frauen-lexikon. Traditionen, Fakten, Perspektiven*, ed. A. Lissner, R. Süssmuth and K. Walter, Freiburg 1988, 1051–9: 1053.

12. According to a 1993 survey by the Allenbach Institute for Demoscopy on 'Women and Church', in the previous ten years the percentage of Catholic women who claimed a 'close connection' with their church declined from 40% to 25% (however, the same thing happened in the Protestant churches). The local church found more sympathy: 43% of all Catholic women and 76% of women with an interest in the church said that they had had 'good experiences' in their parishes, and 69%/80% had 'a good opinion' of their pastors.

13. Cf. R. L. Greaves (ed.), *Triumph over Silence. Women in Protestant History*, Westport, Conn. 1985.

14. In what follows I am going by the excellent survey by G. Scharffenorth and E. Reichle in the articles 'Frau (Neuzeit)' and 'Frauenbewegung', *TRE* XI, 443–67, 471–81. There is also a good deal of material in M. Perrot

(ed.), *Histoire de la vie privée*, Vol. IV, *De la Révolution à la Grande Guerre*, Paris 1987, especially chs II and IV.

15. E. Moltmann-Wendel, 'Christentum und Frauenbewegung in Deutschland', in ead. (ed.), *Frauenbefreiung. Biblische und theologische Argumente*, Munich 1978 (a second, much revised edition of *Menschenrechte für die Frau*, Munich 1974), 13–77: 25.

16. Cf. D. Kaufmann, *Frauen zwischen Aufbruch und Reaktion. Protestantische Frauenbewegung in der ersten Hälfte des 20.Jahrhunderts*, Munich 1988.

17. Two books by Mary Daly, who was at that time still a Catholic theologian, namely *The Church and the Second Sex*, London 1968, and *Beyond God the Father: Towards a Philosophy of Women's Liberation*, Boston 1973, proved provocative when we discussed them in my seminar in 1981.

The scholars, men and women, who supported our 'Women and Christianity project' as an advisory council deserve to be mentioned in a kind of 'Roll of Honour'. They were: Dr Wolfgang Bartholomäus, Professor of Practical Theology at the Catholic Theological Faculty of the University of Tübingen; Dr Kari Elisabeth Børresen, Professor of Church History at the University of Oslo; Dr Gisela Brinker-Gabler, editor of the series 'Women in Society. Texts and Life Stories' published by Fischer Taschenbuch-Verlag, who teaches literature at the University of Cologne; Dr Constance Buchanan, Professor and Director of the Women's Studies Program at Harvard University; Dr Jane D. Douglass, Professor of Church History at the School of Theology in Claremont University California; Dr Andreas Flitner, Professor of Education at the University of Tübingen; Dr Langdon Gilkey, Professor of Systematic Theology at the University of Chicago; Dr Norbert Greinacher, Professor of Practical Theology at the Catholic Theological Faculty of the University of Tübingen; Dr

Catharina J. M. Halkes, Professor and Director of the Institute for Feminism and Christianity at the University of Nijmegen; Dr Andreas Lindt, Professor of Modern Church History at the University of Bern; Dr Dietmar Mieth, Professor of Theological Ethics at the Catholic Theological Faculty of the University of Tübingen; Dr Elisabeth Moltmann-Wendel, freelance writer on women's studies, Tübingen; Dr Jürgen Moltmann, Professor of Systematic Theology at the Protestant Theological Faculty of the University of Tübingen; Dr August Nitschke, Professor of Research into Historical Behaviour at the University of Stuttgart; the Revd Dr Constance Parvey, Director of Studies on the Fellowship of Women and Men in the Church at the World Council of Churches, Geneva, and Bryn Mawr College, Pennsylvania; Dr Helge Pross, Professor of Sociology at Siegen Gesamthochschule; Luise Rinser, writer, Rome; Dr James Robinson, Professor and Director of the Institute for Antiquity and Christianity at Claremont University, California; Dr Alfred Schindler, Professor of Patristics at the University of Bern; Dr Luise Schottroff, Professor of New Testament at the University of Mainz; Dr Elisabeth Schüssler Fiorenza, Professor of New Testament at the University of Notre Dame; Dr Leonard Swidler, Professor of Catholic Theology and Inter-Religious Dialogue at Temple University, Philadelphia, USA; Dr Klaus Thraede, Professor of Classiscal Philology and Archaeology at the University of Regensburg; Dr Angelika Wagner, Professor of Psychology at Reutlingen Pedagogische Hochschule.

18. Moltmann-Wendel, 'Christentum und Frauenbewegung' (n.15), 75. Catharina Halkes, 'Towards a History of Feminist Theology in Europe', in the *Jahrbuch der Europäischen Gesellschaft für die theologische Forschung von Frauen, Feministische Theologie im europäischen Kontext*, eds A. Esser and L. Schottroff, Kampen 1993,

11–37, gives a survey of the most important events, publications and authors of early European feminist theology (1960–75), from Gertrud Heinzelmann and Elisabeth Gössmann through Catharina Halkes, Elisabeth Schüssler Fiorenza and Mary Daly to Kari E. Børresen and Ida Raffling (to mention only the best known). The volume also contains a brief summary of the most important activities and publications since 1945 of the World Council of Churches, which with its consultations and publications – especially *Sexism in the 1970s* (1974) – has made a crucial contribution on the Protestant side to the breakthrough of feminist theological approaches.

19. Cf. B. Hübener and H. Meesmann (eds), *Streitfall Feministische Theologie*, Düsseldorf 1993.

20. Cf. Gal. 3.28.

21. *Publik-Forum*, 16 July 1976.